ARCHAEOLOGICAL SURVEY OF WESTERN INDIA

NOTES

ON THE

BAUDDHA ROCK-TEMPLES OF AJANTA,

THEIR PAINTINGS AND SCULPTURES,

AND

ON THE PAINTINGS OF THE BAGH CAVES, MODERN BAUDDHA MYTHOLOGY,

&c.

ARCHAEOLOGICAL SURVEY OF WESTERN INDIA

NOTES

ON THE

BAUDDHA ROCK-TEMPLES OF AJANTA,

THEIR PAINTINGS AND SCULPTURES,

AND

ON THE PAINTINGS OF THE BAGH CAVES, MODERN BAUDDHA MYTHOLOGY, &c.

BY

J. BURGESS, M.R.A.S., F.R.G.S.,

MEM, DE LA SOC. ASIAT.

ARCHAEOLOGICAL SURVEYOR AND REPORTER TO GOVERNMENT,
WESTERN INDIA

GYAN

Published by

Gyan Publishing House
5, Ansari Road
Daryaganj, New Delhi-110002
Phone: 011-47034999, 9811692060
E-mail: books@gyanbooks.com

Distribution Network
gyanbooks.com
India, USA, Canada, UK, Australia, France

ISBN : 978-81-212-2692-9 (HB)
First Published, 1879

2nd Impression 2021

Printed at: Gyan Press, Delhi.

Notes on the Bauddha Rock-Temples of Ajanta
Author: J. Burgess

No. 9.] **Archaeological Survey of Western India.**

NOTES

ON THE

BAUDDHA ROCK-TEMPLES OF AJANTA,

THEIR PAINTINGS AND SCULPTURES,

AND

ON THE PAINTINGS OF THE BAGH CAVES, MODERN BAUDDHA MYTHOLOGY, &c.

BY

J. BURGESS, M.R.A.S., F.R.G.S., MEM. DE LA SOC. ASIAT.

ARCHÆOLOGICAL SURVEYOR AND REPORTER TO GOVERNMENT, WESTERN INDIA.

Bombay:

PRINTED BY ORDER OF GOVERNMENT AT THE GOVERNMENT CENTRAL PRESS.

1879.

CONTENTS.

ILLUSTRATIONS.

THE ROCK-TEMPLES OF AJANTA AND THEIR WALL-PAINTINGS

Ajaṇṭâ, as is well known, is situated at the head of one of the passages or ghâṭs that lead down from the Indhyâdri hills, dividing the table-land of the Dekhan from Khândesh in the valley of the Tâptî. Four miles W. N. W. of this town are the caves, to which it gives name. They are approached, however, from Fardapur, a small town at the foot of the ghâṭ, and about three and a half miles north-east from them. They are excavated in the face of an almost per-perpendicular scarp of rock, about 250 feet high, sweeping round in a curve of fully a semicircle, and forming the north or outer side of a wild and lonely glen, down which comes a small stream. Above the caves the ravine terminates abruptly in a water-fall of seven leaps, known as the *sât kuṇḍ*, the lower of which may be from 70 to 80 feet high and the others 100 feet more. The caves extend about 600 yards from east to west round the concave wall of amygdaloid trap that hems in the stream on its north or left side, and vary in elevation from about 35 to 100 feet above the bed of the torrent, the lowest being about a third of the arc from the east end, from which extremity the whole series, for purposes of reference, has been numbered. In this enumeration the lowest cave is No. VIII, and next to it, on the left, are two Chaitya-caves, Nos. IX and X, and these with the Vihâras, numbered XII and XIII, are unquestionably the five oldest caves in the group, which contains, in all, some twenty-nine caves. The walls of a considerable number of these have been covered with paintings of very remarkable merit. Unfortunately the damp, bats, natives, and other ignorant visitors have wrought sad ravages among these pictures, and in but in five or six caves there are still fragments left, which, however, are of great age and interest.

From the difficulty of access to them, the Ajaṇṭâ caves were but little visited until within the last thirty-five years. The first Europeans known to have seen them were some officers of the Madras army in 1819. Lieut. (now General Sir) James E. Alexander of the Lancers, on a tour which he made privately through the Nizam's territories in 1824, visited them and sent a short account of them and their wall-paintings to the Royal Asiatic Society, which was published in their *Transactions* in 1829. Captain Gresley and Mr. Ralph were there in 1828, when Dr. J. Bird was sent up by Sir John Malcolm to examine them. Mr. Ralph's lively notice of the paintings appeared in the *Bengal Asiatic Society's Journal* in 1836. Dr. Bird's account was published in his *Historical Researches* (1847) a work in which the erroneousness of the author's opinions on Buddhism is only matched by the inaccuracies of the drawings that illustrate it. An interesting and trustworthy description of them appeared in the *Bombay Courier* in 1839, from Lieut. Blake, and in 1843 Mr. Fergusson laid before the Royal Asiatic Society his paper on the Rock-cut temples of India, about a dozen pages of which is devoted to a critical architectural description of the Ajaṇṭâ caves and their paintings.

This paper first created a lively interest in these remarkable works of art, and early the following year the Royal Asiatic Society brought them to the notice of the Court of Directors of the East India Company, soliciting their "interposition to preserve the caves from all such causes of injury and decay as may be obviated by means within the authority of our Indian Governments." "With reference, also, to the peculiarly perishable nature of the paintings in the caves of Ajaṇṭâ," the Society "was anxious that carefully executed copies of them should be made before it was too late." Such an application was very generously received by the Court, as it well deserved, and in their despatch of 29th May 1844, the Directors wrote out—that "as those drawings are the only authentic records that exist of many of the usages of the people of India at the probable date of their execution, it would no doubt be little creditable to an enlightened government to suffer them to perish without an effort to perpetuate their subjects by faithful and artistic delineation. We therefore recommend it to your special consideration to determine upon and adopt such measures, either by the occasional employment of some of our talented officers, when the calls of the public service permit of it, or by such other means as may appear to you to be best calculated to ensure the procuring of good copies of the paintings in the caves of Ajaṇṭâ and of drawings of the other caves; using such means also for the protection of the caves themselves against delapidation as may be consistent with any use to which they may have been legitimately applied."

As the main result of this despatch Major (then Capt.) R. Gill of the Madras army, an excellent artist, was engaged to make facsimile copies of all the frescoes in the Ajaṇṭâ caves, and allowed adequate assistance. The work occupied several years, till the mutiny, and the copies—thirty or thereabouts in number, many of them of very large size—were sent to London from time to time. All, except the five last executed, were exhibited in the Indian Court of the Sydenham Crystal Palace. There they were destroyed by fire in the latter part of 1866. They were, of course, the labour of years, and it was hoped, they would perpetuate the most interesting portions of the painting that for a long while past had been rapidly decaying. Alas for official wisdom and forethought! no copy, tracing, or photograph, was taken from them before sending them to be exhibited, and finally burnt; and now all that we possess of the work of one of the most faithful of artists are copies in Mrs. Speir's *Ancient India*, on a very small scale indeed,—of two of his pictures and of eight detached fragments from others.

It was exceedingly desirable, however, that another effort should be made to preserve a satisfactory record of them, and that with as little delay as possible, for the effects of the monsoons, bats, and nest-building insects, added to the vandalism of native visitors, was rapidly destroying what was left. Whilst any thing worth copying remains, it was surely very desirable to get exact reproductions of such fragments. When we can read the history of Buddhism, as it is to be found in its immense literature, we cannot doubt but these pictures will throw much light upon it and by-gone times. But if anything was to be done, it ought to be done quickly, for rarely have we seen more palpably the effects of "decay's effacing fingers" than in the havoc made among these unique paintings during the last few years.

With this conviction, application was again made through the Government of Bombay for a small annual grant to be applied to this work, and in 1872 a grant of Rs. 5,000 per annum was sanctioned by the Government of India. Mr. Griffiths, Decorative Artist, in the Bombay School of Art, an officer of the highest artistic ability, was appointed to take charge and began work in December 1873; since which date he has spent four dry weather seasons at the caves with a number of the School-of-Art students copying the frescoes. His copies are regularly sent to England, and placed in the India Museum at Kensington.

In about half the caves there are no remains of painting, and in some that are quite unfinished, there probably never was any, but in some thirteen of them fragments of greater or less extent still exist.

Of the date of these paintings it is difficult to form a very definite estimate, nor are they all of the same age. Over the door, on the inside of the front wall of Cave IX, is a fine fragment, which I take to belong to an earlier date than the major part of the paintings in Caves I, II., &c.; while again on the front wall of Cave I. are two large fragments that seem probably to be of a later date than the others. There are, moreover, in Cave IX some portions of one layer of painting over another, which must be older, probably a good deal older If we attribute the generality of the paintings in Caves I, II, IX, XVI, XVII, .&c., to the sixth century, which we may support by the style of alphabetical character used in a few painted inscriptions and names of figures represented in the paintings, we shall probably not be far wrong. The later pictures may then be attributed to the seventh century, and the earlier ones, in Caves IX and X, may possibly date even as far back as the second—in the time of the later Ândhrabhṛitya kings, the great patrons of Buddhism in the first three centures of our era.

The scenes represented are generally from the legendary history of Buddha and the *Jâtakas*, the visit of Asita to the infant Buddha, the temptation of Buddha by Mâra and his forces, Buddhist miracles, the Jâtaka of king S'ibi, legends of the Nâgas, hunting scenes, battle pieces, the carrying off of the relics to Ceylon, &c., &c. Few of these pieces have ever yet been identified, because no visitor has had the time to spare on the spot and the books at hand to refer to, in order to determine which story each represents. The scenes depicted, too, separately cover a much larger space, and are more complicated, than would at first sight appear to be the case. They are divided, too, into separate acts or sections in a way that is sometimes perplexing. The copies hitherto made are often only of parts of a whole story, and this must be borne in mind by those who use them in attempting to read their contents.

Certain parts of the pictures are always represented conventionally, and it is necessary to note this before further examination. For example: Whenever the scene of any picture is intended to be among the Himâlayas or other mountains, this is indicated by the background being chequered by what might seem to represent bricks, usually with one or two sides of a dark or bluish green and the other light; these are the rocks, presented with a conventionalism worthy of Chinese artists. To interpret the meaning, however, there are frequently represented on these blocks, figures of birds and monkeys, and sometimes of Bhill or other wild tribes of bowmen and the fabled inhabitants of the hills—Kirâtas, Guhyakas, and Kinnaras,—the latter the musicians to the mountain gods, with human busts and the legs and tails of birds. Torrents and trees are also occasionally depicted.

It may be remarked that this mode of representing mountain scenery is employed also in the sculptures,—especially in the favourite one in Brahmanical caves where Râvana is represented under mount Kailâsa trying to carry it off. A small piece of sculpture above the figure of Bhairava Kapâlabhrit at Elephanta, which some antiquarians have tried to interpret as the mystic syllable, ॐ, is nothing more than an indication that the scene is laid among mountains. The same form is repeated again and again in these Ajaṇṭâ frescoes.

Rivers and the sea are equally fantastically drawn, and sometimes with rocky shores. But the fishes, *śaṅkhas*, &c., in them, and a boat generally interpret the representation at once.

Doors and gateways are represented always in one form, as an entrance between two jambs surmounted by a semicircular coping terminating in the chaitya window, ornament at either end, usally a *dwârapâla, darwân*, or *chokidâr*, is represented standing in or near it, but in many cases some other figure is passing in or out and connecting the scene inside with that in the court, street, or champaign.

The palaces or buildings are represented by a flat roof over the heads of the figures, supported by slender pillars, often with blue capitals, and commonly dividing the area within into a central hall and two side aisles or verandahs.

The dresses are very various but pretty clearly distinctive of the classes represented. The great ones—Râjas, Diwâns, and nobles—wear but little clothing at least above the waist, but much jewellery, armlets, necklaces, fillets, and high *mukuṭas*, or crowns. Men of lower rank are often more covered, but have little or no jewelry. Bhikshus and Monks usually are covered by their *śelâ*, or robe, which leaves only the right shoulder bare. Rânis and ladies of distinction, and perhaps also their more personal servants wear much jewellery on their persons, but of different sorts according to their rank. The rânis are frequently, if not always, represented almost as if they were nude; very close examination, however, shows that that is not intended, but that they are dressed in—

"A wondrous work of thin transparent lawn"

—so thin indeed that the painter has failed to depict it, and has usually contented himself by slightly indicating it in a few very light touches of whitish colour across the thighs, and by tracing its flowered border, and painting the chain by which it was held up round the waist.

Dancing women are represented much as they would be now in an abundance of flowing coloured clothing.

Dâsîs and *Kañchukinîs*, household slaves or servants, wear *cholîs* and a *sârî* round the loins—usually of striped cloth.

To these preliminary notes, which might be greatly extended, I shall only add the following extracts from Mr. Griffith's first *Report*:—

"The condition of mind which originated and executed these paintings at Ajaṇṭâ, must have been very similar to that which produced the early Italian paintings of the 14th century, as we find much that is common to both. Little attention paid to the science of art—a general crowding of figures into a subject; regard being had more to the truthful rendering of a story rather than a beautiful rendering of it: not that they discarded beauty, but they did not make it the primary motive for representation. There is a want of aerial perspective, the parts are delicately shaded, not forced by light and shade, giving the whole a look of flatness, a quality to be desired in mural decoration.

"Whoever were the authors of these paintings, they must have constantly mixed with the world. Scenes of every-day life, such as preparing food, carrying water, buying and selling—processions, hunting scenes, elephant fights, men and women engaged in singing, dancing, and playing on musical instruments. Many are most gracefully, and all are most graphically depicted upon these walls; and they could only have been done by men who were constant spectators of such scenes; by men of keen observation and retentive memories. The artists certainly could not have observed one of the ten commandments which Buddha imposed on his disciples, viz., to abstain from public spectacles. In every example that has come under my observation, the action of the hands is admirable, and unmistakeably conveys the particular expression the artist intended.

" Sir Emerson Tennent, in his work on Ceylon, states that the Chinese traveller Fa Hian, who lived in the fifth century of the Christian era, describes the condition of Anurâjapura (in Ceylon) and the ceremonies which took place there :—' The sacred tooth of Buddha was publicly exposed on sacred days in the capital with gorgeous ceremonies which he recounts, and thence carried in procession to the mountains without fear, the road to which was perfumed and decked with flowers for the occasion ; and the festival was concluded by a dramatic representation of events in the life of Buddha, illustrated by scenery and costumes, with figures of elephants and stags so delicately coloured as to be undistinguishable from nature.' The fact of men taking part in, and witnessing such sights as described above, will account in some measure for the processional scenes which are painted on the walls of Ajaṇṭâ."

Proceeding now to a detailed description of these caves and what is left of their remarkable wall-paintings. Let us begin with cave I, and take each cave in order.

CAVE I.

Cave I is one of the finest *Vihâras* of the kind. Certainly no vihâra at Ajaṇṭâ has been so handsomely ornamented as this one. In front of the verandah there has been a porch, supported by two advanced columns, of which only fragments of the bases and elegant capitals remain : at each end, outside the verandah, there is a room whose open front is supported by two pillars, the floors being raised a few steps in order that the elaborate entablature of the façade might be carried round the whole front at the same level. The room on the east opens into another, nearly 13½ feet square, and all but perfectly dark ; that on the left opens into two others somewhat smaller. Now, mark the six columns and two pilasters of the verandah. The pair in the middle, which originally formed part of the porch, like all the others, have square bases and elaborately carved bracket capitals. Above the bases, they are first octagonal, then there is a belt of 16 faces, above which they are fluted with bands of beautifully elaborate tracery up to the thick compressed cushion between two fillets, on which rests the carved facia under the capital. The next pillars on either side are similarly rich in carving, but have narrower bands of tracery round the upper portion of the fluting, and their flutes are spiral. Outside these are two octagonal pillars with three bands of tracery round them, supporting a very deep, square, carved facia under the bracket capital. The pilasters beyond these have short, fluted necks with tracery above and below them—more like what we should work in metal than attempt in stone. The central compartment in each capital has its own group of human figures.

The wings of the brackets of the columns are ornamented with *Gandharvas* and *Apsarâs*, the central panels with figures of Buddha and his worshippers ; but on the sixth pillar it is apparently a version of the temptation of Mâra. On his left are two females. On his right, a man is shooting at him with a bow, another above, in a peaked cap, is in the attitude of throwing a stone at him.

The façade of the cave is the only instance here of a vihâra decorated with sculpture.

The entablature is broken over the porch and the projecting rooms at the end; but, in order that it might run round in parallel lines—besides the contrivance of raising the floors of the smaller rooms outside—an architrave has been introduced over each of the side chapels, ornamented with representations of the horse-shoe form window of the Chaitya-caves, each enclosing figures.

The architrave all along the front is sculptured; above each column there is a compartment containing human figures only; at the corners are terminal figures apparently intended for lions or *Śârdûlas*; and the remaining spaces are filled principally with elephants in every variety of attitude, and cut with great spirit and correctness.

The part over the front of the porch has been mostly destroyed when the pillars gave way, but from a fragment that remains, the lower frieze or architrave seems to have been filled with groups of figures, possibly scenes from the life of Buddha. The left side is carved with elephants fighting, and with the figure of a rider on a *Śârdûla* at the corners. Continuing the same member along the façade to the left, we have, after the usual corner *Śârdûla*, two figures beating drums and one playing on some sort of flute followed by others with Nepalese swords, oblong shields, three figures on horseback, one blowing a long trumpet, then three elephants and another horse with their riders. The next to the left is an in-door scene—a râja and his wife in earnest converse with three attendants. Outside a saddled horse is being led out towards a tree, and to the left a little figure carrying a bag on his back towards two figures sitting talking under foliage with birds in it. Beyond these a male elephant stands facing a man sitting at the foot of a tree with a stick in his hand. Then comes another in-door scene in which the wife has her arms round her husband's neck and two female household servants (*dâsîs*) stand by. Outside are four elephants, the first butting against a tree, the next, a young one, following its dam, who is pinning a tiger to the ground; the fourth is behind, and has apparently turned tail. Then come two buffaloes at strife, a man behind each urging it on. To the left are other two human figures in front of the corner *Śârdûla*.

This band is continued across the front of the left side chapel (Plate IV. fig. 1). To the left of the corner *Śârdûla* are four figures, a woman, a man with a stick or sword, another with a shield, and a figure sitting on the ground. Towards these comes Buddha in his chariot with two horses and the driver. Next is a royal figure seated on a seat in a garden under a tree, while a woman plays on a musical instrument to him, and another waits on him behind. A palm tree separates this from the next scene, in which Buddha is driving to the left, and passing a plantain tree, meets an aged man with a staff. Behind him is Buddha in his car again and just before it some men carrying a dead body and a woman wailing by it. The rock is here broken, but to the left we have a royal figure seated again on an *âsana* with attendants, and a horse looking in at him; beyond is a man walking out, and, after another defaced piece, a horse with an attendant beside it. This sculpture then represents the signs which led to Siddhartha, afterwards the Buddha, becoming an ascetic, and his escape.

On the right side of the porch, the sculpture is a representation of a hunt of the wild ox, spiritedly carved. On the front of the façade, to the right of it, is another hunting scene, perhaps of deer; the first horseman on the left is spearing one, and by the side of the next runs a dog or cheetah. Behind are three elephants with riders, followed by a fat ill-proportioned figure, bearing some load at the ends of a pole over his shoulder. In the next compartment is a domestic scene,—a stout squatting figure with a cup in his hand, caressed by his wife, behind whom stands a servant with a flagon.

To the right of this is an out-door scene,—first an elephant, before whom a man sits as if feeding it or addressing it, while beyond him another stands with a staff in his left hand. A woman proceeds to the right with a vessel on her left hand, towards a man who squats under a tree addressing another woman, who kneels before him in an attitude of supplication. Behind her is a dwarf with a bag on his back, and beside it a man leading a saddled horse, behind which stands another man holding an umbrella, probably the attendants of the kneeling woman.

Another small compartment to the right of this represents a râja and his wife seated together, attended by two female servants.

The next contains six wild elephants, the first two fighting and the next dragging a huge snake in his trunk; then a *Śârdûla* terminates the front. Over the right side chapel the continuation begins as usual with the *Śârdûla*, in front of a group of cattle, to the right of which are two figures seated, and beyond them is seen the head of a bearded old man. Then, under trees, are two more men with beards and their hair done up in the *jaṭâ* style of devotees: behind them a third head is seen. One has a bottle and beside the other the same vessel is hung in the tripod stand represented in front of the dying Buddha in Cave XXVI, and elsewhere. Another bearded ascetic is leaving these, with something like a club in his right hand and a bent rod over his left shoulder. He is meeting a man who appears to address him, but to the right is another with an uplifted sword as if about to strike this last. To the right is a plantain tree and a saddled horse led by a man.

The second compartment is a small interior scene in which a man sits listening to a lady attended by two female servants.

The last compartment is broken, but began with a kneeling figure offering some present to a portly man seated.

Above the entablature is a projecting band, carved with representations of the Chaitya window, each containing a human head; then comes a frieze, ornamented with compartments, containing human pairs, in different attitudes attended by female servants. These are separated by spaces filled with figures of the sacred goose (*haṅsa*)—in varieties of position, with the wings extended into elaborate floriated tracery so as to fill the spaces—a device well known in Singhalese art; and on the Buddhist carvings of Ceylon we find the elephant and the *haṅsa* constantly occurring, whilst the latter also figures on the standard of Burma. Above this frieze is a line of tigers' heads, then a dentilated fillet, then another with a line of string tracery, surmounted by a belt, containing human heads within miniatures of the Chaitya window, each with the hair represented as if a sort of heavy wig.

The verandah is about 64 feet long by 9¼ wide and 13½ high, and has a chamber at each end. A wide door in the centre, with elaborately carved jambs and entablature, leads into the great hall, and there are smaller doors near each end and two windows. The great hall, or *śâlâ*, is nearly 64 feet square, and its roof is supported by a colonnade of twenty pillars, leaving an aisle of about 9½ feet wide all round. The columns are about 5½ feet apart; but the middle ones on each side of the square are 6½ feet asunder. Their bases are about 2¾ feet square, and with the four pilasters in continuation of the front and back row are mostly very elaborately carved.

The front of the brackets in the first row of columns in the hall, and the inner sides of all the rest are carved; the inner side of the front row and those that face the side and back aisles have been painted with similar figures, and Mr. Griffiths has copied almost the only one of the latter that is left fairly entire, in his painting No. 104. It is an excellent representation of two bulls fighting.

The sculptures on the other sides of these brackets may be briefly noticed. The wings of the brackets are very much alike: of those facing the front aisle, the two central, and two corner pillars have *Śardûlas* or horned lions with riders; the other two pillars have elephants with two riders on each of those that face the inner area of the hall; the two central ones on each side have an *Apsara* and *Gandharva*; and the others a human figure coming out of the mouth of a *makara*, except that the first column on the left side has two fat figures on each wing, and the fourth *Vidyâdharas*. The central panels are more varied. In the two middle pillars in the front row are figures worshipping a *Dahgoba;* in the pair outside these is a small fat figure (in one case carrying a load) under an arch *(toraṇa)* thrown over him between the mouths of two *makaras;* in the corner pair, is Buddha seated in the usual fashion between two *chaurî*-bearers; in the middle area of the hall the two central columns on the right hand have, in this position, four deer so arranged that one head serves for any one of the four,—a curious conceit which seems to have been in favour with the early Hindu sculptors, as we find similar combinations elsewhere; the panels of the brackets on each side these have elephants fighting. The left central pillar on the left hand has a râja, his wife and child, diwân, two *châmara* bearers and an attendant, perhaps, Suddhodana and Mayadêvî with the infant Buddha; and on the right hand one, two râjas seated, with attendants—much as in the two chapels of Cave II. The first pillar in the left row has an eight-armed fat dwarf attended by two others, one of them probably a Nâga figure; in the fourth, two Nâga râjas are worshipping the *Dahgoba.* In the back row, the two central columns have Nâga figures with their Nâgakanyâs worshipping richly decorated Dahgobas; on the first pillar, to the left hand, are two half human figures with a lotus flower between them, and on the fourth, two deer with the wheel between them—the usual *chinha* of Buddha.

The most elaborate description would convey but a faint idea of the rich tracery and sculpture on the shafts of the back row of pillars: above the base they are ornamented by mythological *makaras* or dragons; the upper part of the shaft is encircled by a deep belt of the most elaborate tracery, in which are wrought medallions containing human figures; the facia above is supported at the corners by dwarfs. Again, on the left side, on the corners of the bases, we find the *makara* and dwarf together, and on eight facets round the upper part of the columns are pairs of rampant antelopes, bridled by garlands held in the mouths of grinning faces between each pair. The corner pillars have three brackets each. On each side of the cave there are five cells or *gṛihas* for the monks, and in the back four—two on each side of the shrine.

In the middle of the back are two pillars with brackets of human figures, and between these we pass into an antechamber, about 10 feet by 9, leading into a shrine, about 20 feet square, in which is a colossal statue of Buddha with a figure of Indra at each side as his supporters, wearing rich head dresses (*mukuṭas*), and their hair in curls. That on Buddha's left has the *vajra*, or thunderbolt, in his left hand. The wheel in front of the throne is set edgewise, as with the Jainas, between two deer, with three worshippers on Buddha's left and five on his right, behind the deer.

The Paintings in Cave I.

The whole cave has been painted, though near the floor, it has entirely disappeared. Within the last fourteen years much of the painting in this and in all the caves has either fallen off or been wantonly defaced; yet there are some as interesting fragments in this as in any other cave, and much of it has already been faithfully copied by Mr. Griffiths.

I.

Commencing with the left end of the front aisle[1] :—The painting here has been much destroyed, but it appears that a band, about 8 inches deep above the cell-door, cut off the upper scene from those on each side, which are almost entirely gone, except two female heads on the right, an arm, and part of a red-skinned figure.

Above the door is a scene which can still be made out.[2] Near the centre, in a palace, represented in the usual conventional way, is a Nâga-râja seated on ablue cushion[2] his head overshadowed by the *pañcha-phaṇa-chhatra* or five hooded canopy, while his *rânî*, with a single hood over her head, sits almost in his lap, dressed in the usual almost invisible garments worn by ladies of exalted rank, the rich flowered border only of her transparent vesture is seen passing across her thighs, while she looks round in his face. He holds in his right hand some green object like a cup, while his left rests on the shoulder of his queen. A woman servant or *dâsî*, in blue clothing, with many bracelets of a simple pattern on her arms, chafes the feet of her mistress, and looks to the right. On the rânî's left a red-skinned female holds up her left hand, with a fan or *pankha*, and looks up and away from the râja. A fair-skinned one in a thin close-fitting dress, marked with a flowered pattern, and with her hair in a white napkin (like the Parsi women) bends forward towards the royal pair with what look like a pair of chopsticks in her right hand, and carrying in her left a vessel. Behind her is a dark red-skinned woman and another, who looks round to the right, as does also the first-mentioned attendant, at a person of distinction dressed in a blue and gray or gold garment "ornamented with scrolls, stars, birds, and the ox," covering his whole person, and with a cloth over the head, who enters on the right, as if for an interview. A woman behind him leans against a pillar and also looks at him while apparently playing on pair of cymbals. Beyond the red-skinned female is a man looking upwards and perhaps playing on a stringed instrument. Among these women their manner of dressing the hair is varied and fanciful "some are holding their curly locks in their hands."[3]

---

[1] For arrangements of these pictures on the walls, on Plate I.

[2] This is Mr. Griffiths's copy, marked 'V'.

[3] I had written out these notes on the paintings before perusing Mr. Griffiths's account of those of them he has copied; on comparing his descriptions afterwards, I adopted portions of them, marking the extracts always with inverted commas.

At the râja's right hand sits a female servant, and behind him stands a woman with a *châmara* or *chaurî*, while an old man enters from the left, somewhat stout, and with a bald or shaven head.

In a building behind this man is seen a ladder or stair and a person ascending it.

Outside the palace, on the right, a fair face looks round a pillar; the back view of a rânî richly jewelled, appears above, looking over her right shoulder and holding a wand in her left hand, and fragments of other figures, but principally dresses, connect this with the right corner, where a lady of rank highly bejewelled rests her elbow daintily on a pillow and looks out to the left. Behind her is a sofa, or the dress of a dancing girl or a *kañchukinî*. The rest is destroyed.

On this picture Mr. Griffiths makes the following remarks in his report:—

"The polychromatic decoration of the architecture is fairly represented. The general colour of the wall is green, divided by horizontal bands of red filled in with scroll and leaf ornament in gray. These bands are further emphasised by a border on either side of the fillet and bead ornament. The shafts of the pillars are divided by ornamental bands into three distinct divisions—the upper and lower are coloured, as if intended to represent marble or granite, while the middle are mottled blue. The ceiling is blue, as are also some of the long bottle-shaped caps, upon which are placed cushion-shaped members, coloured similar to the upper and lower divisions of the shafts.

"Immediately above and behind the râja is shown a partly opened door.

"The method of wearing the *dhôtî*, and more especially the decoration and colour of the material forming it, running in horizontal bands, as seen in this and other compositions, resemble in a remarkable manner, a similar article of clothing as worn in Nêpal and Burma at the present day.

"This painting, together with others that have already been copied, afford unmistakable evidence of the existance of made dresses, cut and sewn to fit the body, and further ornamented by means of embroidery."

II.

Covering a portion of the wall to the right of the pilaster adjoining the last, is an open air and mountain scene, doubtless some legendary story that may be identified by those who have read the Pâli *Jâtakas*. In a mountain cave in the upper left corner sits a Buddha, and before him a râja on a cushion, who makes obeisance to the Buddha, while behind him is his rânî and a red-skinned attendant. In front of the rânî, at the râja's left hand, a dwarf, in a short striped kirtle, brings forward a green box, and in front, between the râja and Buddha, sits a woman holding her hand to her hair.

To the right of this group a red man seems to have hold of a great snake,[1] while further to the right, seven men pull at a cord fastened to his teeth or tongue, and two others stand beside them. Before the man grasping the body of the snake, are six oxen. To the left, and below the râja, a man holds some object in his hand, and still further to the left a Nâga Râja with seven hoods, leads

[1] This portion of the scene is depicted in one of the five copies preserved of Major Gill's series.

a man (like the one holding the snake) to the edge of a pool and seems enticing him to go in with him. It must be remembered that the story of these Nâga people is that they lived in lakes as water-snakes, and only assumed the human form when they appeared among men.

III.

The next scene[1] extends from between the first and second cell-doors, but above their lintels, to the right side of the third :—

A râja and rânî sit in their palace, and before them two servants. Behind the rânî is a female attendant with a *châmara*, and behind the râja a red-skinned one ; while another of lighter complexion brings in a vessel with flowers. In the verandah, to the right, are three more women, one apparently bringing in news. To the right again,[2] under a maṇḍap, is a draped dancing woman, exhibiting her elbows in the approved fashion. Two on the left of her play flutes (*vaṅśi*). One on the other side, plays on two large standing drums (*mṛidaṅga*). Two have small cymbals, and one stands behind to the left looking on, while two are seated in front,—one with the *ravája* the other with the *ḍúka*—a long drum very narrow in the middle. To the right is the conventional gateway, out of which the râja proceeds on a light coloured elephant ; before him is, perhaps, his *diwán* and the *Yuvarâja* on horseback, the latter, also, with an umbrella (*chattra*) borne over him. A green and a chesnut horse, the latter prancing,[3] appear in the crowd. The soldiers of the retinue have long blue Nepalese swords, slightly crooked and broad near the point ; one has a shield, and one a spear, and three carry standards with oval discs at the top of the shafts.

The procession seems to turn round to its left towards the upper part of the picture and then back to the left where a Yogi sits with a blue band across his knees for support and a *rudrâksha mâlâ* or rosary in his hand. The horses and elephant—the latter covered with a tiger's skin—stand on the extreme right of the picture,[4] and the râja and his retinue dismounted appear before the Yogi, where all the principal figures that appear below can be identified. The Yuvarája makes profound obeisance to the Yogi, at whose[5] left side are two blue-coloured deer and a *haṅsa* (or sacred goose). A disciple, perhaps, in white clothing stands behind, and two laics, with joined hands, below and before him.

Below the palace of the râja an inner apartment is represented, in which a woman rolls out something on a flat stone or board, with several dishes beside her. To the right another is raising her right hand as if listening to or looking out for something, while in her other hand she holds a vessel. Still to the right is a third female. Below are three sipâhis, one with a Nepalese sword, one with a bow and quiver, and the third with a spear.

---

[1] Part of this scene is in Major Gill's copy referred to above.

[2] Another of Major Gill's copies begins with this part of the scene and continues it to the right.

[3] The figure in front, who looks up as if alarmed, is represented as a woman in Major Gill's copy : the original has suffered since it was taken, but it is probable from the earrings that this is right. She holds a spear.

[4] These lie outside to the right of the copy made by Major Gill.

[5] When the pronouns *his*, *her*, *whose*, are used, the right or left hand of the person represented is meant. 'The right' and 'the left' indicate the spectator's right and left respectively.

On the right side of the cell-door is the remains of, perhaps, another part of the scene, but all that is left is a striped conical object, possibly the top of a tent.

IV.

The next scene may be regarded as beginning above the third cell-door and seems to be continued up to the back pilaster.

Commencing at the front, or left hand side, we have râja seated in his palace and in front of him, on another seat, his rânî richly jewelled, and with a striped *sârî* round her loins, who is earnestly talking with him. Behind him, to the left, is a very fair woman, and behind her again a reddish one, both with *chamaras*. In front of these a lady, with jewels and a kirtle, talks to another, and a servant beside them seems to listen. At the râja's right foot sits another servant. Beyond the rânî, a fair woman with lemon-shaped eyes stands with a *pankha* over her shoulder, and a second listening, while looking round the back of the rânî's seat, a third stares with widely opened eyes and grasps the cushion. Behind these, to the right, a fourth woman listens to a fifth coming in at the door, who by the gesture of the hands, seems to lay off some startling news.

Outside the door, the râja, with the *chhatra* borne over him, and his diwân, mounted on horse-back are going out, accompanied by their retinue. To the right is the sea shore, and those who reach it point to the water, and look back, as if telling the râja something. On the sea are two boats; in the first the people are at their ease, and a râja under a *chhatra* sits near the stern. The other boat has made shipwreck, for the water with fishes in it is flowing across it. One man is in the water with terror painted on his face, apparently lest the fish should swallow him, or a horrible monster, and sea bull which are represented in front of the boat, while below are shells. Another man in the boat raises his hands in despair. The picture may be intended to mean that the râja having heard of a wreck went out in his own ship to the rescue.

On the extreme right, beyond the sea, are two men walking behind some plaintain trees, and lower down is a man (possibly the one represented in the sinking boat above) sitting and receiving some present from another.

Below the latter portion of this picture a Nâga Râja sits in an interior and four people beside him. Outside is a man, apparently in deep grief, appealing to another, and behind him is a Râkshasa, or demon-monster, who appears to be doing deadly harm to a figure of which only the foot remains.

Between the third and fourth doors on this wall is the top of a *rath*, or large car, with at least four people inside, one in the right side with a rich *mukuṭa*, while outside, to the right, is a *chaurî*-bearer, and two others with curly hair; one of them also wearing a high *mukuṭa*; then four more heads, two of females, one being very fair; and still to the right, two more looking in the opposite direction,—one holding an umbrella over a rânî, who looks down towards two smaller heads below.[1]

V.

The next scene[2] is on the back wall; and on the left end of it a râja in his palace is seated on a square *sinhâsana* with a high carved back, receiving his

---

[1] Major Gill's copies extend only to the left side of the third cell-door, and as the rest is still pretty entire, it is to be hoped it will be copied soon.

[2] The greater part of this is preserved for us in third of Major Gill's copies at South Kensington.

abhisheka, or anointing. A green female presents to him a dish of flowers, and behind her stands a *chaurî*-bearer and another; while two men behind with white cloths round their hair, pour the *abhisheka* upon him from large round *kûmbhas* or vases.

In another division of the palace, to the left, a man with his hair in a white cloth, and wearing a striped *dhôtî*, brings in a large water-pot on his shoulder, and another in front of him, with a white sleeved jacket and short red and white striped drawers, leans upon a stick, looking towards the râja. Up the steps, in front, a boy proceeds with a large round dish on his head, from which a young woman, apparently nude, lifts out something. Beyond her, another female with striped kirtle, takes a plate of flowers in to the râja. Behind the pillar, separating the apartments, a green female plies the *chaurî* over the râja. Outside this second apartment are four Bhikshus stretching out their hands for the alms usual on such an occasion,—one of them with an umbrella, and another with the *jaṭâ* or head-dress of a devotee. Beyond them are plantain trees.

To the left of this again, is another building in which sits a Buddha or other devotee with his alms bowl in his lap, and above him, in a niche of the wall, some earthenware vessels. In another apartment, to the left, are four women in the dress of nobility: one kneels as if making some mark on the ground; another holds a basin with some offering for the devotee. To the left, in a third apartment,[1] behind these ladies, a râja is seated with some attendants; but the painting here is too much defaced for description. Below the first part of this scene is an interior in which a man followed by his wife or other woman, presents, in a salver, four human heads to a Bhikshu—not a Bauddha one—who seemingly refuses them; and to the right he is represented again as departing. Three other people look on.

At the left end of this wall, between the last cell-door and the corner, is a portion of a scene, in which, from four windows, as many females and one man are looking out on some sight below, now entirely destroyed.

In the end of the back aisle no portion of the painting is left.

VI.

To the right of No. 5 and between it and the left side of the antechamber is a mountain scene, in which the tall central figure is perhaps Śakra or Indra, a favourite personage with the Buddhists.[2] Here he is represented as somewhat fair with a high jewelled crown, or *mukuṭa*, a blue water-lily in his right hand and wearing the Brahmanical *upavîta* or sacred cord, made of strings of pearls. About his loins is a striped *dhôtî*. On his left stands his consort *Sachî*,—much darker than Indra, and so—according to native ideas—more beautiful;[3] she wears a *dhôtî* similar to his, has a flower in her right hand, a high *mukuṭa* or crown, and turns her face a little to the left. Between the two appears a figure standing behind

---

[1] This does not appear in Major Gill's copy.

[2] This scene is on the fourth of Major Gill's copies at South Kensington.

[3] Observe this in the language too *Syâma*, originally meaning black or dark, being now applied to young or fresh.

in close fitting blue clothes and also with a high crown, but not so richly jewelled as the other two, and holding the *châmara.*

Close to Indra's right leg are two figures, the first with the features of a female, and behind them is a *vetrî* or *chobdâr*, holding a sceptre or rod. Above Indra's left shoulder is a monkey climbing up the rocks and a bird (*chakrawâka*); above are two others but larger and of blue colour, and behind them, among foliage, a *Gandharva*, apparently pouring something into a cup in his left hand, whilst his *Apsarâ* leans on his right shoulder.

On the other side are a monkey approaching a pair of *Guhyakas* (cave dwellers) seated on a rock, and behind them a pair of *Kinnaras*,—those strange conceptions of the heavenly musicians, represented with human head and bust, and the tail feathers and legs of a bird, the male here playing on the *ravâja*, or guitar, and the female on small cymbals, with a cloud behind them. A little below and to the left of these, a pair are seated together also on a rock, the lady in the transparent vesture betokening high rank, and only indicated by her *mêkhlâ*, her husband looking over her right shoulder. Behind are monkeys climbing up the rocks, and above are a *Yaksha* with long straight sword and small shield, and his consert behind him floating on the clouds, while just before him is another celestial personage. High up in the extreme left is a lion, pretty well represented.

VII.

On the left end of the antechamber is the representation of Buddha, beset by the emissaries of *Mâra*—a favourite subject with the Buddhists.

Mr. Griffiths has copied this picture,[1] and his description of it is so complete that it here produced almost *verbatim*:—

"This picture when complete occupied the whole left wall of the antechamber to the sanctuary, 12 feet 9 by 8 feet 4½; but a portion has been entirely destroyed, *i.e.*, 1 foot from the top and 3 feet 5 inches from the bottom."

"In the centre of the picture, on a raised green dais" "is Buddha, seated in the usual manner, with folded limbs, and the right hand extended. He wears his Kaśâya robe and a nimbus," (*bhâmaṇḍala*) "appears behind his head, above which foliage may be traced, probably the Bodhi tree. On Buddha's right is a woman, probably a daughter of Mâra, half reclining against the dais, on which her left hand rests; while her right is extended in a very expressive manner as she addresses Buddha. Behind her" and a little higher "is a long curly-haired warrior in a striped waist-cloth (*dhôti*), and a kind of cloak loosely tied round the neck and floating in the air behind him. In his right hand is a long straight sword, while his left arm is extended to its full length, and the hand bent back at right angles to it, as if in the act of warning Buddha. Above this figure is a *Râkshasa* with the little finger of each hand thrust well into the corners of the mouth, the others drawing down the eyelids, reminding us of children's efforts at making 'Bogie faces.' On its head is perched an owl," the symbol of destruction, and in the Râkshasa's "ear a small blue bell. Behind this figure is what appears to be a tiger,

[1] This is marked 'X' in his copies of 1875-76.

with its head well thrown up and ridden by a figure dressed in a blue chequered *dhôti*, the upper portion of the figure is destroyed. Next to this is a green figure with a horse's head, holding a club in its right hand. A little behind and below is (*Kâlî*,) a thin guant old hag-like figure with long pendant breasts and ribs well developed. Her left arm is extended as if hurling defiance at Buddha, while in her right hand she holds a quaintly carved hatchet-shaped instrument, and has a tiger skin thrown round her waist. She is a very good representative of the 'old witch' of popular tradition. In front of her is the figure of a warrior, with a long straight sword," who appears to carry over his left shoulder, making "desperate efforts to get at Buddha. Directly below him is a very impish-looking face, and next we have a figure with a pig's head, holding a large ornamental club. Below are three figures in a line, the first is of a green colour, and is turning away from the fray, possibly under the conviction that further effort is useless, while the second entertaining the opposite opinion, is in the act of gathering up all his strength to hurl a javelin at Buddha. The third, with curiously formed head-dress of a skull, and what appear to be blue feathers, is also aiming a javelin, and pointing with the finger of the left hand to Buddha. Immediately below this figures is one of a bearded warrior (all the others have shaven chins) clad in a tight fitting yellow coat, under which is a blue garment, with a belt in which he carries a dagger. A striped blue shawl is tied round the neck. On the left arm he carries a large shield, and in his right hand he flourishes a blue scimitar. A wreath decorates his hair. Next is a figure represented as having just discharged an arrow at Buddha. Below are two figures too indistinct to be described.

"Proceeding to the group of figures on the right of the picture: immediately on Buddha's left is a female occupying nearly a similar position to the one on the other side, but the attitude is more constrained and less graceful and natural than its companion. Behind her" and above on the picture "is a warrior in a striped and chequered waist-cloth (*dhôtî*), with a thin band round the belly, a kind of shawl tied round the neck, the ends of which float behind. He is aiming a blow with a club at Buddha. Then," between him and Buddha, "comes another large 'bogie-face,' with huge mouth, teeth, and eyes." Above this is a very ghastly looking face with a blue snake issuing from its mouth. Beside it is a figure with a blue-striped *dhôtî*, in the act of hurling a spear at Buddha. Next to it is another figure with a pig's head, having in its right hand a straight sword, and in his left a small circular shield. The row of figures above is very indistinct, but portions of two are visible, one green, and the other an animal with large open mouth and sleepy eye, similar in position to the tiger on the opposite side.

"On the right, midway down the picture, is a richly bejewelled Prince (Mâra). A figure to his left holds over him the ennobling umbrella (*chhatra*), while below a dwarf (*gaṇa*) is carrying a standard, composed partly of a peacock's feather, the other part is unintelligible. To the Prince's right, and looking up into his face, is another dwarf, significantly displaying an empty quiver. The Prince is in the act of walking away from Buddha. And from his action and the expression of his face, I take him to be the personification of Mâra, who finding that his evil influences and devices have fallen powerless on Buddha, turns away deeply mortified, exclaiming 'how is it that I, who am able to hold in my power both Śakra and all the other Dêvas, have been defeated with all my host of followers by this Śaman of the Śâkya race.' I am undecided as to the intention of the green figure behind, whether it is to cut down the Prince in front or whether in his attempt to thrust at Buddha, his sword has clung to his hand, as the legend describes. In the corner below are portions of figures depicted in a state of terror at the noise and confusion of the scene above. One is turning away and stopping his ears with both his hands. Another figure has a small tortoise shaped ornament suspended from the neck.

"Below Buddha, in front, are the women (two of them remarkable for a redundancy of jewellery and a scarcity of clothing), whom Mâra Râja bade use all their wiles to induce Buddha to relent and give way to his passions. 'In obedience to their lord's command, they went with mincing gait towards the spot where the Bôdhisattva sat beneath the tree, and standing at a short distance from him, they proceeded to put into practice every ogling way and lascivious art they could. Some with dainty smiles to display their white teeth, some with eyes askance looking at Bôdhisattva; others stooping down before him and looking upwards into his face; others drooping their heads so as to conceal their faces, and looking at one another; others with their hands toying with their breasts; other half uncovered with their breasts and hips bare; others again entirely nude, walking to and fro, with their heads turning this way and that, and their eyes darting side glances. But, notwithstanding all these temptations, Bôdhisattva remained unchanged in face, and appearance—tranquil, and at perfect rest he sat—even as the full moon when it emerges from the hands of Râhu, the Asura Râja, pure and spotless; or the sun when first he scatters his dazzling rays to the morning; or as the lily that reposes on the placid waters; or as the brightness of the flame; firm as Mount Sumeru, so Bôdhisattva was unmoved; even as the iron walls that surround the universe, without the least agitation, his heart and his mind at perfect rest, without fear or anxiety, and entirely self-possessed.'"

VIII.

To the right and left of the shrine-door are two scenes which are only slight variations of one another. Both are laid among the mountains, with a large male figure in the middle, almost certainly Indra, for on the right side of the door may be seen his *vajra* or thunderbolt, in his left hand, and his consort Sachî by his side. On the left side,[1] as remarked by Mr. Griffiths, we have more of the large figure (Indra) depicted than on the right. He is represented with the high jewelled *mukuṭa* or crown, large necklace, earrings, bracelets, armlets, like those represented on some of the figures at Elephanta—twisted twice round the arm in a spiral direction and open at the ends,—and an *upavîta* or sacred cord formed of several strands of pearls twisted together and hung over the left shoulder. "He has a small *dhôti* round the loins, held up by a jewelled waist-belt, and in the right hand he holds a string of flowers. He has a dreamy, meditative expression, and the general contour of the figure differs little from the slim narrow-waisted Hindu of the present day.'"

To the left is a woman (*Sachî*) with a tray of flowers, but, as Mr. Griffiths remarks, "the action is not nearly so graceful or so well rendered" on the left as on the right side of the door. Below "we find the little female dwarf" as on the other side, with upward gaze, holding in her right hand, apparently, a bracelet. On the same level, but to the right of the large figure, is a fragment of another

[1] This is Mr. Griffiths's picture, marked 'Z.'

dwarf. At the top left-hand corner of the picture are a man and woman seated on a kind of platform, well grouped and composed—the graceful delicate action of the woman being remarkably well expressed. Over her limbs is thrown a thin gauze covering, terminating in a blue border; and to judge by this, India appears to have been capable, then, of manufacturing gauze as delicate in texture as the world-wide famed 'Dacca' of the present day. This subject appears to have been a favourite one with the artists; for beside being again repeated in this cave, we meet with it in several of the others. Beside this group will be observed fragments of two birds" (*chakrawâkas*), "and to the right are two figures, male and female; the former, apparently, is in the act of salutation, while the latter is carrying some flowers. Below is a portion of two small" (*Guhyakas*) "rollicking figures. On a level with the head of the large figure to the left are a man and a woman standing behind a wall. While he leans on his left hand on the top of the wall, with the right arm bent, and with the hand directing attention to the large figure, she peeps coyly from behind his back with her left hand resting on his shoulder. Below we have the two birds in a niche, similar in action to those on the other side, but differing in colours, being blue here."

The painting on the right side of the door[1] is very similar with differences of detail. In it we have the upper portion of Indra again, "larger than life with an elaborate jewelled head-dress, a necklace of pearls and blue stones. The left arm is bent, and in the hand is the blue thunderbolt (*vajra*). Below to the right" is his consort Sachî, "remarkably well drawn and depicted in a most graceful attitude, holding daintily, with both hands, a tray, made either of rope or twisted reeds, containing flowers, of which a large, white lotus" (*kamala*) "partly open, is here seen. She is attired in the costume usually met with in the paintings. Besides her is a female dwarf, who is gazing upwards, with partly opened mouth, at the large figure just described. Depending from its left hand is a casket resembling an incensory."

Behind this group is the conventional representation of the mountain "interspersed with foliage, birds, and figures in pairs. In the right hand corner a man and woman are represented seated, the former is playing on a stringed instrument, and the latter on cymbals. Below are two figures"—(*Kirâtas* or mountaineers)—"behind a wall, represented as if in the act of listening. The one with his foot resting over the top of the wall, holds in his left hand a bow and two arrows, and the other carries a small bag. In a small niche in the wall, just below, are two birds, reddish in colour."

On the left side, nearly on a level with the upper two of these figures, stands a man, to whom a woman offers a vessel containing flowers, and high up on the same side is a *Gandharva* (or part of one) floating in the clouds with a vessel and flowers in it.

IX.

On the right hand wall of the antechamber are a large number of painted Buddhas with the nimbus (*bhâmaṇḍala*) round their heads, mostly seated, but some standing on lotos flowers, the leaves and stalks being shewn in all the vacant spaces. Mr. Griffiths has copied a portion of this wall, measuring 7 feet by 4,[2] comprising eight figures and parts of three others. He remarks that—"the delicate foliage which fills in the spaces between the figures will give some

[1] This is Mr. Griffiths's picture, marked 'Y.'

[2] This is his picture, marked 'O.'

idea of the power of these old artists as designers, and also of their knowledge of the growth of plants."

X.

Between the front of the antechamber and the first cell-door to the right, is a scene in a mountain[1] represented in the usual conventional style. In the centre is a colossal figure of a râja with richly jewelled *mukuṭa* or crown, holding a flower in his right hand and leaning his left on the shoulder of an attendant, whose left hand passes through a black leather strap which comes over his shoulder and supports a long straight sword at his back, the ends of the strap being fastened by a buckle. This man has a chain about his neck. Behind him is a tall female figure, perhaps a *chamara*-bearer, and above to the right is part of a sitting figure with his legs crossed.

At the râja's right side is—perhaps the Yuvarâja, or heir-apparent (distinguishable by his crown), bringing forward and offering a trayful of flowers. Between the râja and him, a bald-head is thrust forward from behind—perhaps that of a eunuch (*kañchukî*), who is richly dressed, and rests his chin upon his right hand. In front of him, and to the left, are two ladies in the dress of *rânîs*, with coronets on their head, leaving the presence, one with a tray of flowers, looking wistfully back.

On this picture Mr. Griffiths makes the following remarks :—

"I would especially call attention to the drawing of the heads of the two women in the left hand corner, and the portion of the woman's face and arm on the right, additional interest attaches to this picture, from the fact that nearly all the ornaments which were used to adorn the person are here in a very good state of preservation, and are most admirably drawn, especially the twist that is given to the string of pearls on the colossal figure and those round the neck of the woman in the left hand corner, and the chain round the neck of the figure to the right, with an accidental hitch in it. I would also call attention to the drawing of the long-pointed nails of the same figure and also those of the colossal figure. Many of the bracelets differ little in design from those now worn, and the white wreaths of flowers in the hair of the woman are similarly worn by native women of the present day."

XI.

Over the two cell-doors in this back wall is a large scene.[2] Towards the right of the picture, over the second cell-door, a râja sits in his palace, with a pillow of blue and gold at his back, and leans forward as if looking intently at, if not speaking to a man with a large snake (*nâga*), which rises from a basket at the lower right hand corner of this part of the scene. Between the râja and the man with the snake is seen a stout red-skinned man, perhaps a diwân, and over the râja's left shoulder is seen a female servant, probably a *pankhâwalî* ; behind the diwân is another figure, and to the right of him is seated the Rânî, with her hair falling on her shoulders, her left hand resting on her raised knee, and her right raised towards her chin, while she looks enquiringly towards the râja. Behind her are three men standing, one with a *talwâr* (or sword), and in front, to the left, are two seated, one with a moustache,—and all apparently listening to the conversation.

---

[1] This is Mr. Griffiths's picture 'M.'

[2] Mr. Griffiths's copy is marked 'P.'

In the lower right hand corner is the snake-charmer seated, who has just opened a basket, out of which rises the *nâga*, to which he speaks (and who is perhaps the Nâga Râja in the scene below, but in another *rûpa* or form).[1] To the left, behind the râja, are—a woman with a *châmara*, a man, and—more in front—a woman wearing a *chôlî* or boddice and striped kirtle, pushing forward a boy. Behind are indications of the scene being in a hill with trees.

To the left of this is another portion of the scene, perhaps an antecedent part of the story. In a palace, seated on a stuffed seat with quilted cover and pillow, the blue ends of which are seen behind him, is a râja of rather dark clayey colour, resting his right hand on his queen's leg, who is seated on a similar chair beside him, and to whom he speaks. On the other side is a reddish female dwarf in striped blue loin-cloth, or short kirtle, presenting something (perhaps sweetmeats) on a tray. Behind her is a woman holding strings of jewellery in her hand, and behind a pillar a female is seated gazing on the râja. Out of doors, to the left, is a tall female and a very fair-skinned boy to whom she seems to beckon.

XII.

Below this last and between the cell-doors in this wall, is another in-door scene[2] and a very animated one it is (see Plate III.) The two prominent figures in it are a Nâga Râja, on the left with the five-hooded snake overshadowing his head, and on the right another royal-like personage, seated on a large draped couch, talking interestedly. The Nâga Râja seems to be speaking and to the left is a female with *châmara*. Her hair and that of the principal figures are all three bound with fillets. Behind the Nâga King is a dark red attendant with a straight sword, the richly-jewelled hilt held up, and then a female holding a chased casket in her left hand and a jewel with a string of pearls depending from it in her right. Next to her, and behind the second speaker, is a man with blue and gold flowered robe, and an Iranian head-dress, also holding a sword with blue hilt. At the Nâga Râja's left side sits a female in blue and white striped kirtle, the face turned up and the left hand stretched forward as if speaking or calling attention to something she had to say. Behind the other râja one female is handing a tray with flowers in it to another, and in front of the second a third brings in another flat vessel covered with flowers and leans forward as if listening. Behind this last stands an old man, very fair skinned, with wrinkled brow, and white hair. In front, on the left, are two ladies seated and listening with interest. Most of the females in this picture have their hair hanging in ringlets.

Outside the door-way, to the left, a râja is departing, with high *mukuṭa* on his head and the *chhatra* or state umbralla borne over him, and with him is another figure with a large *pañcha-phaṇa nâga chhatra* over his head. Beyond them are two elephants, one with a rider having the *ankuśa* in his hand.

"Parts of this picture," Mr. Griffiths's remarks, "are admirably executed. In addition to the natural grace and ease with which she is standing, the drawing of the woman holding a casket in one hand and a jewel with a string of pearls from it in the other, is most delicately and truly rendered. The same applies to

---

[1] Mr. Griffiths seems to think he holds the body of the snake with his hand; but the snake is of a much lighter colour, and what his hand rests on is so perfectly circular that I can only regard it as the either cover of the basket out of which the snake rises, or more probably a flat drum like a tambourine, used by snake charmers, and on which he beats with his left hand.

[2] This is the picture of which Mr. Griffiths's copy is indicated by the letter 'N.'

the women seated on the ground in the left hand corner. The upward gaze and sweet expression of the mouth are beautifully given. The left hand of the same woman, which, by the way, I did not discover until I had been at work for some weeks, is drawn with great subtlety and tenderness."

XIII.

To the right of the second cell-door is a picture[1] that seems to be related to the last. The dresses are very nearly, if not quite the same, and some of the figures seem to be identical. It is also a palace scene, in which four of the seven figures left have the snake hood (*śeshaphaṇa*) over their heads,—three females, each having one hood, and one five. Their hair falls down in ringlets, held back in some cases by a fillet. On the left is the Nâga Râja, and beside him sits another without the hoods, but over his head a bearer behind holds the *chhatra*. A Nâga figure, with a single hood and loose hair, stands a little behind and seems to be receiving a long straight sword of state from a female still more to the right and also with a *naga* hood and long ringlets, who holds it up to him by the scabbard, whilst apparently speaking to the others. Before her, and either kneeling or sitting, is a lady of rank[2] looking importuningly at the face of the râja. Behind her is still another *nâgakanyâ*, and in front of her is a portion of one more.

"The porch behind," as Mr. Griffiths remarks, "with the partly open door, is a very fair piece of perspective."

XIV.

The painting on the right wall is so destroyed by holes made in it by bats as almost to defy description.

Above, between the second and third cell-doors, and cut off from the next portion by a white gate-way is a large scene much destroyed. Above are eight elephants. In front have been numerous soldiers, one on horseback, one green-skinned,[3] dressed in striped *dhôtîs* and armed with the long crooked Nepalese swords. Three figures have deep collars round their necks, and all advance towards the left, led apparently by a Râkshasa. In front of them are four or more wild elephants without any housings. Then in a hill scene, Buddha is seated with his feet down, two stand before him in the garb of Bhikshus, and behind him a disciple (*Śishya*) or Bhikshu, stands talking to a man who may be some Sâdhu in white garment, and who offers him a *kalaśa* or vessel. Beside him is a female—also in white dress.

XV.

Over the first cell-door in this right wall, a light-complexioned râja and his wife sit upon a throne, a woman appears in front, female servants behind, and to the right, in a door, two people stand looking out. On the left side is another door from which also a man is looking. To the left of this, are fragments of a scene in which have been numerous men with short hair, one has a necklace and earring, and one wears a white *chadar*.

---

[1] Mr. Griffiths's copy of this is designated by 'Q'—*Report*, 1874-75.

[2] She holds the right hand a little forward, with the thumb pressed against the fore-finger, her left is raised towards her ear.

[3] Can it be that these green people are intended to represent the lower castes?

XVI.

In the right end of the front aisle, over the cell-door, is a large fragment of painting.[1] To the left side sits a râja with *nâga* hood on a seat covered with green cloth (and with little carved suppliants at each side of it), holding one hand up as if addressing the audience. Behind him, to the left, is a tall female leaning against a pillar of the hall, wearing a kirtle of striped stuff like the Gujarât *panch-patta* silk. At her left hand is a reddish-skinned dwarf, *dâsî*, or servant girl, and before her sits another woman with a fly-flap or *chaurî*, wearing a striped loin-cloth, and holding the fore-finger of her left hand to her chin as if pleased, while she looks up towards the right. Near her, and beside the râja's foot-stool (*pâda-pîṭha*) is his spittoon. To the right, and on a lower level than the râja, sits a man, perhaps his diwân, with whom he seems to be conversing; while on a green cushion, at a higher level, sits the queen, in transparent gauze, with rich necklaces of single and twisted chains, and jewelled *mêkhalâ* round her loins. Behind her stands a tall female with a *chaurî* in her right hand, and clothed from the loins to the knee in a vertically striped stuff. Behind, and seen between these, is a fair skinned person, with very simple head-dress, holding a vessel,—perhaps a milkmaid. Behind this and beyond the rânî is another female. Over the diwân's head is seen another with flowers in her left hand and a hand *pankhâ* (or mirror ?) in her right.

Before the rânî sit a very short man and woman, probably servants; the latter with a basket or bag on her shoulder.

On this part of the picture Mr. Griffiths remarks that,—"the artist appears to have had rather a vague notion as to the relative distances of the figures in the picture. For instance, the queen is represented as being in front of the woman, who is seated on the floor between her and the râja, where, according to the laws of perspective, she could not possibly be.

"It is curious to observe the fondness these old painters had for introducing dwarfs into their compositions, and to find the same in pictures by Paul Veronese. In this picture, in the left hand corner, is a female dwarf, holding a small round jar.

"The woman behind the râja is using a small hand *pankhâ*," and holding some object in her left hand. "The portly, disproportionate *chaurî*-bearer on the right is extremely ill drawn. A green curtain is drawn at the back, similar to those used in Europe in the Mediæval age, and which afterwards became an element of decoration so common in Gothic art."

To the right, over the cell-door, is one of the conventional gateways with a lattice window in the side of it and in the recess of it a *kalaśa*, on the top of which is a green ball or a cup turned with its mouth down.

Beyond this, to the right, is a pastoral scene with a herd of cows of different colours—two cows and a calf, green—some lying, others standing. Behind them stand two green demons, and a third figure, as if about to carry them off. Much of this portion has been destroyed.

"The bovine characteristics of the animals." Mr. Griffiths notes "are remarkably well expressed, and this part of the composition is very like Albert

---

[1] This has been copied by Mr. Griffiths as 'W' of his series, *Report for* 1875-76. Possibly it is connected with the story of No. 1 in the other end of the same aisle.

Durer's work. Above are fragments of three figures; the centre one of the ordinary complexion; the ones on either side are green, and are probably intended for goblins or *Râkshasas.* The one on the left has a red bottle in the left hand."

Below, to the left of the cell-door, has been another picture, now all destroyed, except the square canopy of a *siñhâsana* or throne, with short strings of pearls hung from its edges, the centre being of striped silk.

XVII.

The painting on the front wall has been much destroyed, and what was left has been, especially of late years, much holed by bats.

Between the window on the right, and the central door is a large piece,[1] differing from any yet described in the inferiority of style and the different physiognomy and dress. It is probably fully half a century later than the rest.

A pale-skinned Râja sits in Darbâr on a cushion placed on a dais, higher than usual, with a semicircle of green over the middle of the back of it, behind his head, and having a gilt border with little *vidyâdhara* figures on each side of it, and *makara's* mouths at the corners of the back. From the right three fair bearded men in Iranian costume, with peaked caps and completely clothed, approach him in crouching attitude; the first bearing a string of pearls; the second a jug or bottle (of wine perhaps); and the third a large tray filled with presents. Behind the third stands another figure near the door in white clothing, perhaps the porter, with a stick in his hand and a dagger in his belt, apparently speaking to another Iranian in the doorway, bringing in some present. Behind the porter is another foreigner in full white clothing, with stockings, curled hair and peaked cap, holding a vessel in his hands, and with a long straight sword at his back.

Behind the throne stand an attendant and a female with *châmara*; to the right of her a reddish fair figure in blue clothes; and beside him one still fairer with a rich head-dress and striped loin-cloth holding a green stick. In front of him is a stool, broad at the upper and lower ends (*bhadrâsana*); and to the right are a red and a fair man, the latter with his arms crossed on his breast and wearing a red turban. In front of him is a reddish-skinned man, his left hand on his knee while he bends forward and holds up the fingers of the right hand, as if addressing some information to the râja: probably he is the interpreter. Beyond him, to the right, are other two figures, one having in his hand a dish, perhaps with fruit, and a spear with a small flag attached to it.

In front of the three Iranians, sit three royally dressed figures, perhaps members of the royal family (*Râja kumâras*), the reddish one in the centre, perhaps the Yuvarâja. To the left of them is a man with a basket, and in front of the throne a woman sits with a *châmara*, and beside her is an elegantly chased spittoon.

On the left, at the proper right side of the throne, sits another lady with rich head-dress a 'breast-band', a basket beside her and some object in her lap. Behind her is a short female or dwarf, of red complexion, with blue earring, and not so richly dressed. Behind these two again is a third richly dressed young woman with breast-band also, and looking towards the râja. Above is a fourth with a *châmara*, while a fifth face looks over the back of the throne on the râja's right.

---

[1] This is Mr. Griffiths's copy, 'S.' of 1875-76.

Outside the palace, to the right, an Iranian, like the one seen in the door, appears speaking to a green man with a stick in his hand. Behind are two horses, and in front of them a *sipâhi* or soldier with a sword.

A portion to the left of this interesting memento of some embassy from Persia, probably in the seventh century, is completely destroyed.

Below are some indistinct figures in small compartments, not very intelligible.

XVIII.

In a similar position, on the other side of the door, is another fragment,[1] probably of about the same age. Above the left of the centre of the picture a râja with a blue and white bird in his lap sits, on a low dais, with a high back,—(the *sângamanchi* of Kachh and Kâthiâwâd). Behind it is seen the faces of two attendants; and then to the right a female *chaurî*-bearer. Below, a dark curly haired boy brings forward a jug. To the left, in front of the râja, are two females, one with a vessel or casket and her hair tied up in a chignon (*veṇî* Mar. *ambaḍa*); and sitting on the floor with crossed arms and looking up, is a child to whom he seems to speak. In another apartment, to the right, is a clay-coloured individual with jewelled head-dress, and a green-skinned companion with a long nose, both looking at the râja.

Outside, to the right, is a pîpal tree, and beyond it, in front of a building, a râja (to judge by his head-dress, and probably the same as in the last part of the picture) with striped drawers, holds the cord of one of a pair of scales in which he has placed his left foot. Behind him, on his left, is a man in white clothes with a rod in his hand, and three figures from the other end of the beam look on, from clouds—hence they must be *dêvas* witnessing some event of great importance.

To the left of the râja are five women; the one in front with a child towards which he stretches his hand as if to take it to put in the scale. The women seem to object to this,—one fair, another of greenish complexion beating their breasts. "Behind these two, is one with a very ruddy complexion wearing a striped *sâḍî*. She is directing an appealing look to the prince, her right hand rests on her breast, and the left holds by one arm the obstreperous child below, whose yells are attracting the attention of the woman seated in front, probably his mother. The general pose of this figure is most graceful and natural. Beside her is seated another woman with a pathetic expression of face, who is holding a child on her lap with both hands. Behind this group of women rises a betel-nut palm (*areca catechu*), and a group of large leaved foliage, the young clusters of brown leaves contrasting favourably with the older green ones,—another example of the truthfulness of these old artists in representing natural facts. Behind the scales, to the right of the prince, is a ruddy figure with a white skull cap and close fitting white coat (*angarka*) and *kamarband* arranged in three distinct rolls. He is saluting the prince with his right hand and carrying a staff in the left. Overlooking a wall behind the râja two red-bearded men with their hair done up like Yogîs seem to speak to the prince. Above these are fragments of two standing figures and next is one sitting cross-legged, apparently in conversation with two figures, likewise seated to the right, one of

---

[1] This is Mr. Griffiths's copy, 'T.' of 1875-76.

whom is of a greenish colour and the other is represented with the palms of his hands brought together in front as a mark of respect, a custom universal among the natives of India at the present day when seated in the presence of and being addressed by a superior. These figures are seated upon rectangular blocks of some undistinguishable substance."

Below the first described scene the râja again appears together with the little boy, apparently at the *aśrama* of some Yogîs, where an old shaven-headed Yogî meets him, while behind stand five disciples with a cloth each over his left shoulder. The first of these holds a water vessel or *kalaśa*, and with the other hand signals to the râja, apparently to stop. To the right of these are two red-bearded Yogîs near a jungle, the one with flowers the other with *kuśa* grass. Part of another figure can be made out, but the rest to the right is much destroyed.

XIX.

From above the left window to the end of the front aisle are a series of scenes that were probably all connected, but parts of them are so defaced that they cannot be easily if at all satisfactorily made out.

Over the window[1] is a female figure (perhaps Mayadêvî) reclining on a couch and looking downwards towards a *dâsî* who has her hand on the lady's necklace as if removing it. Another to the right with flowered *chôlî* or boddice has a *chaurî* (or a mop ?) At the head of the couch a fair female servant holds a large *kalaśa*, pouring its contents on her mistress's head, as does another to the right, with only a blue and white loin-cloth and rich necklace, on her limbs. Beyond the couch one fully covered holds a stick as if for defence. To the right of all and a little lower, in the door-way, is another servant with a large vessel having a spout on one side of it.

To the right of this again, the same lady is seated in a palace, in the transparent robe of royalty, with a slave at her right hand. Two women stand behind and a third (a *kañchukinî*) covered, sits talking with her. Further to the right, and lower, a man is seated, perhaps an astrologer; his person covered with a flowered cloth, apparently addressing the lady. Behind him, but nearer to her mistress, is a very fair woman with a large flat dish or tray, on which are some objects which she seems about to offer to this man. Behind these, to the right, a man in a white dress comes in by the door which divides this from the next part of the picture.

Below is a defaced fragment with two figures in it.

Above to the right again we have another episode in which the lady and her *kañchukinî* are seated together; while behind the lady another woman comes in holding out her hand, her lips apart and eyes wide open as if in astonishment. A pillar of the palace separates this from what follows.

Here a large piece of plaster out of the centre, hinders a satisfactory reading of the picture.

On the left is a half nude *chaurî*-woman. To the right is the head and hand of another attendant holding a rod, both looking towards a figure with rich pearl *upavitâ*, now destroyed. Behind him a lady, perhaps the same as in

---

1 This portion is on Mr. Griffiths's copy, marked 'R' of 1874-75.

2 Mr. Griffiths's copy, marked 'V' of 1875-76.

the other scenes, leans forward, looking up to the left. Beyond and behind her an attendant in dark *chôlî* with white flowers on it, also looks in the same direction as the first two, while behind and lower, at the left side of the lady, are other two servants in white clothes. A plantain palm indicates the open air on the right, and beyond this some female figures can be only partially made out.

Over this from the window to within 18 inches of the wall is the only piece of ceiling fresco left in this aisle. It contains chiefly fruit and flowers in small compartments, but one contains two figures in Persian dress.

XX.—*The Ceiling (Plate II).*

I cannot do better here than transcribe Mr. Griffiths's account of the ceiling[1] and how he copied it. "Although a great portion of this ceiling is destroyed," he remarks, "yet enough remains to give us the general arrangement of the whole. At first sight it appears very complicated in design, but after a little study it will be seen how simply the whole thing is arranged. Adhering to the idea of imitating their wooden originals, which idea pervades everything they did here, the Buddhists, in decorating this ceiling, merely adopted the principal divisions formed by the several timbers in one of their wooden floors. In fact, the plan of the ceiling is nothing more than the plan of a wooden-floor taken from below; or to put it plainer, if another floor were added to the present cave, the timbers, which would enter into the construction of that floor, on looking up at them from below, would be represented by the principal lines on this ceiling. Taking one unit of the ceiling and reducing it to its simple constructive lines, we shall find it to be made up of a plan of four columns *a, a, a, a*, with connecting girders *b, b, b, b*. Across these run joists *c, c, c, c*, and at right angles to these again are smaller joists *d, d, d, d*. The space is thus divided into a number of panels, varying in shape and filled with ornament. This principle of division is carried out in every painted ceiling that still remains of the Vihâra Caves at Ajaṇṭâ, with one exception only, and that is in Cave No. XVII, where the principal arrangement consists of circles. To show that this principle is no fanciful idea of my own," a plan of "a portion of the ceiling in the aisle of Cave No. XVI, where the construction is cut out of the solid rock would be similar to that of No. I. This ancient system of flooring is used up to the present day without any modification."

"Having divided the ceiling into a number of panels by the method shown above, with a circle for variety in the central division, we find these panels filled with ornaments of such variety and beauty, where we have naturalism and conventionalism so harmoniously combined as to call forth our highest admiration. For delicate colouring, variety in design, flow of line, and filling of space, I think they are unequalled. Although every panel has been thought out, and not a touch in one carelessly given, yet the whole work bears the impression of having been done with the greatest ease and freedom, not only freedom of execution, but also freedom of thought as a reference to the copies made will testify.

"The ornament in the smaller squares is painted alternately on a black and red ground. The ground colour was first laid in, and then the ornament was

---

[1] See Plate II. where, however, the letter *a, a, a, a, b, b, &c.*, have been omitted for sake of clearness: these can easily be supplied. The numbers are those attached to the different panels as copied by Mr. Griffiths, from whose drawing this has been copied.

painted solidly over this in white. It was further developed by thin, transparent colours over the white.

"In order fully[1] to appreciate the copies of the paintings, it is necessary to bear in mind that the originals were designed and painted, to occupy certain fixed positions and were seen in a subdued light. Many of the copies of the panels, on close inspection, appear coarse and unfinished; but seen at their proper distance (never less than 7 feet from the spectator) apparent coarseness assumes a delicate gradation."

On three of the panels[1] of this ceiling Dr. Rajendralâl Mitra has commented at considerable length in the *Journal of the Asiatic Society of Bengal*, vol. XLVII. (1878), pp. 68-72, reproducing two of them in lithography as "Bactrian Domestic Scenes." The ribbon ends, triangular-shaped streamers, or banderoles, behind the shoulders of the figures, and which are repeated almost invariably where similar figures are introduced, as they frequently are elsewhere, are alone sufficient to mark them as Iranian or Sassanian, rather than Baktrian, and they are a characteristic mark on Sassanian coins. Dr. Rajendralâl considers these panels as "three editions" of the same scene and describes them thus:—

"In its simplest version it represents a diwân placed in front of a cloth-screen, and covered with cushions and a check-pattern coverlet, and on it are seated a big, stout, burly-looking man and a lady by his side. The man is seated cross-legged, and is in an amatory mood, perhaps somewhat befuddled with wine. His face is heavy and square, and he has both a beard and moustache. He wears long hair, covered by a thick conical cap with a turban, or a fur band around it, like the Qilpáq cap of the Central Asiatic races of the present day. On his body is a coat or tunic reaching to the knee and trimmed with what appears to me, patch-work decorations; knee-breeches and striped stockings complete his dress. He holds a cup in his left hand, and before him, on the ground, in front of the diwân, there is a covered tray. The lady beside him has a gown reaching to the knee, a shell jacket (both set off with patch-work trimmings), and a pair of striped stockings. She has a skull-cap on her head, and earrings. Her right hand is lifted as in the act of telling something interesting to her lord. To the right of the man, in front of the diwân, there stands a maid arrayed in a long flowing gown, which leaves only the tips of her shoes visible, and holds a flagon, shaped like a sodawater bottle with a long narrow neck, ready to replenish the cup of her lord. Behind the mistress there is a second maid with a wide-mouthed covered jar in her hand.

"In the second version the man holds the cup in his right hand and a stick or straight sword in his left. He has also an elaborately-worked belt, and the trimmings of the coat and gowns are of different patterns. The lady leans on the shoulder of her lord by her right hand, and by her attitude expresses great solicitude to please him. There is also a third maid, squatting in front and ready to serve out edibles from the covered tray beside her.

"The third version (No. 4) is even more developed. The screen behind the diwân is set off with floral designs. The coat of the hero and the gown of his lady, and also that of her maid, are set off with triangular striped streamers flying from the back. The features of the lady are vivid with life, and the expression of

---

[1] Nos. 4, 20, and 64: Plate IV, fig. 2, represents No. 4.

endearment on her face is truly admirable. The second maid holds a *surahi*, or goglet, instead of a jar. The lady has, instead of a cap, a fillet round her head with an aigrette in front, and the maids similar fillets, but without the jewel. The third maid is replaced by two bearded, thick-lipped Negro-looking servants, who are serving out dishes from the covered tray. The stockings in the last two versions are white. In two small panels the male figure is reproduced in company with another male,—two jovial companions, engaged in pledging their faith to each other over a cup of liquor. The striped stockings are distinctly seen in these, as also a pair of check-pattern trousers, not striped."

The figures in these scenes, however, are evidently Sassanian or Persian, not Baktrian, as Dr. Rajendralâl supposes.

His paper closes with a curious *non sequitur* as to the age of these paintings. If I understand the author's argument it is this,—' Mr. Fergusson regards the earliest cave here as not later than the second century B. C., and the latest are supposed to be of the 5th or 6th century: accepting these data, the paintings in Cave I.' (perhaps the *latest* in the group) " represent phases of Indian life from eighteen hundred to two thousand years ago."

Now the data seem to indicate that if Cave I. was excavated in the fifth or sixth century, as is probable, the paintings in it, which are of two distinct eras, cannot be older than twelve on thirteen hundred years. The wall scene No. 17 above, which he carefully describes as the reception of a Persian embassy (pp. 62—68) is later than most of the wall-painting, and can hardly be earlier than the seventh century, and the ceilings all about one age, may at earliest, belong to the end of the sixth, and may be as late as the early part of the seventh.

CAVE II.

Cave II. is another Vihâra, similar to No. I., but smaller and somewhat different in the style of its front columns. The verandah is 46¼ feet in length, supported in front by four pillars and two pilasters, all of the same style, having a torus and fillet at the base, but no plinth; to about a fourth up they have 16 sides, above they have 32 flutes with belts of elaborate tracery. The capitals are flower-shaped, along which the flutes of the column are continued as petals: first there is a deep calyx, widest near the bottom and terminating in a double row of petals; then, above a very small fillet, there is a thick projecting torus, surmounted by a bell-shaped flower of about the same depth as the torus, and on this rests a thin plain abacus. Over them runs a plain architrave on which the roof rests, and beyond which it projects very considerably, with indications of the patterns in which it was once painted. At each end of the verandah are chambers similar to those in Cave I,—the architrave above the pillars in front of them being filled with carving. In the central compartment of the façade of the chapel in the right end of the verandah is a *Nâga Râja* and attendants. In that on the left end is a female and child. The side compartments in both are occupied by fat male figures. Each chapel opens into an inner cell. At the left end of the façade in a niche, is Buddha squatting in the *dharma-chakra mudrâ* and over each shoulder is a smaller one. The cave has two windows, and a fine central door with an elaborate architrave, at the bottom of which are *dwarpâlas* with five hooded snake canopies, each apparently holding a flower; above this, the compartments on each side are filled with pairs of standing figures, male and female, in varied attitudes; above the door the figures are sitting ones, with a single fat one in the centre compartment. Outside the architrave are three members of florid tracery, then a pilaster, similar in style to the columns, and surmounted by a female figure standing under the foliage of a tree and leaning on a dwarf. Over the upper architrave is a line of prostrate figures with what resembles a crown in the centre.

The hall inside is 47 feet 7 inches wide, by 48 feet 4 inches deep, and is supported by twelve pillars, similar to those in the last cave, the most highly ornamented being those just in front of the sanctuary. These pillars are very similar to those in Cave I. Those in the front row and the central pair in the back row have little fat dwarfs with four arms supporting the corners of the square caps. The central pairs of pillars in the back and front rows are the richest in carving, and the corner ones have flutes running in spirals up two belts of the shaft. The brackets have *Vidyâdharas* and *Apsarâs* on the projections. In the central panels of the brackets in the back row are numbers of people worshipping the Dahgoba; in those of the right side row are single fat figures canopied by *toraṇas* rising from the mouths of *makaras*; and in the rest a fat râja, his wife, and other female attendants. The pilasters are beautifully carved. In a line with the side aisles in the back wall, there are chambers with two pillars and pilasters in their fronts.

In the chamber on the right, or east, side of the sanctuary, are sculptured a pair of portly sitting figures, (Plate VI.) both with rich head-dresses: the woman holds a child on her knee, apparently amusing it with a toy held in her right hand; to the right and left of them are female slaves with *chaurîs*, whilst one behind holds a parrot and fruit. Below are eleven small figures, some of them making rams butt, others wrestling, and some playing on musical instruments for the child's amusement. This is probably intended to represent the infancy of Buddha nursed by his mother Mayâdêvî (or Gautamî) with a peculiar round head-dress, sitting by his father, Suddhodana. In the upper corners are representations of a holy man (perhaps Asita) giving instructions—probably to the same pair with their child.

In a corresponding apartment on the other side there are two fat male figures with elaborate head-dresses, neck-chains and armlets, the one holding an egg-shaped object in his hand. The frilled back to the head-dress on the right hand figure is of the style in vogue in sculptures of about the fifth or sixth century A.D. Female slaves with *chauris* stand on either side, and *Gandharvas* or Buddhist cherubs with large wigs appear in the upper corners. Below are two semicircular representations; but whether intended for vegetable food or not, we cannot say. Over the fronts of these side chapels in the back wall are also sculptured groups, the central one over the left chapel having a Nâga Râja and his family in it.

The shrine itself is about 14 feet by 11; but, owing to the cave being only 11 feet 5 inches high, it is very dark, and smells strongly of bats. The Buddha squats in the *dharma-chakra mudrâ* with the wheel and two deer in front, and behind them, to the right, a female in the attitude of adoration before a male with a long object like an empty bag;—to the left is a female kneeling with a long-twisted object, and behind her a kneeling male worshipper. The right *châmara*-bearer is richly dressed with *mukuṭa* and nimbus, the left one is Avalôkitêśvara and has the *jaṭâ* head-dress and in his left hand a bottle-shaped object.

THE PAINTINGS IN CAVE II.

Though much decayed, the paintings in this Cave have suffered less during the last few years than those in other caves. But the bats have recently attacked the ceiling and will soon ruin it, unless shut out. It is the only cave that retains any of the painting in the shrine.

I.—*The Verandah Ceiling.*

Much of the beautifully decorated ceiling still remains in such a state that the pattern can be made out completely. When entire, it must have been remarkably beautiful and delicate, both in colour and design. Mr. Griffiths has copied several panels and half the central compartment. The spandrils of the latter, he says, "are admirably designed, the one on the left with two floating figures, a man and a woman; the one on the right with two men wrestling, terminating from the waist in conventional scroll work. Half of this spandril is drawn in red, and appears to have been left incomplete, although its diagonal is treated in a similar way, half green and half grey. The diagonal spandril to the floating figures is entirely destroyed. The wreath of leaves and flowers speaks for itself." These panels he regards as "admirable specimens of ornamental art filled in with parrots, the blue and white lotos, and other flowers and fruits." Some small panels in it only have been damaged within recent years.

II.

Mr. Griffiths very justly remarks that "the little that remains of the painting in the verandah of this cave is enough to show that it was of a very high order as regards design, drawing, and colour. Taking into consideration the fact that the whole of the verandah is exposed to all changes of weather, from the extreme moisture of the monsoon to the intense dry heat of the hot season with its accompanying hot winds, it is remarkable how well the colours have stood this trying ordeal. The blues are as vivid now as they were the day they were put on."

The back wall of the verandah, however, has suffered much. The three fragments that remain have been copied by Mr. Griffiths, and his descriptions of two of them are so correct that I transcribe them with only a few verbal alterations.

The first fragment is between the door and the left window in the verandah. [1] "On the extreme left, in the upper corner," are two *Arhats* on clouds, having a slightly redder cast of skin than the other figures in this composition. "They are clad alike in simple garments worn like a woman's *sâḍî* thrown over the left shoulder, one being of a green striped material and the other gray. The hair is gathered up into a tuft at the back of the head with a few tresses streaming gracefully round it. The true rendering of hair is one of the most difficult things in the province of art. In these two figures it is extremely well designed and executed. Both figures have not a vestige of jewellery." "The foremost has the hands represented in the act of begging, adoring, or saluting; whom—it is difficult to make out. The two portions of figures below are in a very dilapidated state. The one to the left has a decidedly Egyptian cast of expression, the figure—whether man or woman, it is difficult to say, probably the latter—appears to be putting on ornaments; one hand is seen near the ear, whilst the eyes are directed to a looking glass, which is being held by an attendant. To the right, next in order, are two, one male and the other female, very perfect illustrations of those quaint little creatures, half human, half bird formation," called *Kinnaras*. The male is playing a blue flute and the female blue cymbals. They are standing on conventional rocks. "Above these are two figures, one a man and the other a woman. The man, who is highly bejewelled and whose curly locks of hair fall gracefully around the head, holds in his right hand a blue lily, whilst the left rests on the right shoulder of the woman, who is dressed in a blue *chôlî* and carries in her hands a leaf-full of flowers. The strip of blue below is a fragment of a large sword."

"Proceeding to the right, we have the head and shoulders of a colossal" regal "figure, the ornamental head-dress of which is admirably drawn." Above are two *Kirâtas* "peeping from behind" the rocks. "The delicate brushed-up moustache of the lower is curious. This figure is appealing to the one above him, pointing down with the right hand, apparently to the colossal figure below, whilst holding in his left a bow and two arrows. These old artists were such keen observers of nature that the smallest detail did not escape their observation, for we see painted the plugs which are inserted in the punctures in the lobe of the ear to prevent them closing. Next in order," and on clouds, is a male (*Yaksha*) "with a blue sword in the right hand, whilst the left supports the back of his female consort" or *Apasarâ*, who is reclining on a green ledge of rock. "Her right elbow is resting on the man's shoulder with the fore-arm doubled forward; her left hand is slightly raised to meet the right. Behind are what appear to be white and blue clouds. The old man" leaning to the right "below with the well-drawn head sparsely covered with a few gray hairs, the ear admirably rendered, and the drawing of the shoulder and back well understood, makes one regret that so little is left of him." In front is a woman.

[1] This is the picture marked 'A.'—*Report for* 1874-75.

III.

The second fragment [1] is to the right of the door, and contains little more than "two floating figures," a *Yaksha*, "with a long thin sword in the right hand and a small shield in the left, is supporting a female" an *Apsarâ*, "whose form is beautifully rounded in the original. Below can be traced a fragment of a turban and a well-drawn hand."

IV.

In the third fragment,[2] which is at the right end of the verandah between the window and the wall, we have, on the left, two *Arhats* or Bauddha devotees, who have attained to the power of flying on the clouds, and on the right a *Gandharva* or *Devata* and an *Apsarâ*, with a regal figure, perhaps of Indra, in the middle with high ornamental head-dress, to the left is Sachî, his wife, "and to the right a green coloured *châmara*-bearer vigorously applying it." These green-skinned people possibly represent people of the Śudra caste, and occur frequently in the paintings.

V.

In the chapel, at the right end of the verandah, are some fragments of painting. On the left wall, at the upper left corner, a Râja sits upon his throne with his feet on a stool, and two women with *châmaras* attend him. To the right are a number of men carrying a sort of palanquin or bier with two poles. Before it are three soldiers, one with a very long shield. In front, a light coloured man with a sword prostrates himself towards the palanquin or else towards a green man in white drawers in front of it, who, with a reddish old man, are approaching a large dark green tree. In the right corner of the room the palanquin is again presented in the jungle, placed on the ground, and a lady sits beside it as if drowsy or deeply engaged in thought. To the left of the palanquin three people are lying asleep, and a fourth—a female—looks out of it in astonishment or terror.

Above the palanquin, to the right, is a child, and a green man (or woman) sits looking at it, while it lies by the side of a conventionalized representation of a lake full of *kamala* flowers, geese, &c.

Below is a *Nâga Râja* with five hoods and his *Nâga Kanyâ* with one hood, seated on a throne. Behind him are two other *Nâga Kanyâs* and a third in front and below the pond. The rest is destroyed.

VI.

To the right of the cell-door, in the same apartment, can be traced an elephant and a horse.

On the right hand wall are also a few traces of painting; among them a râja on his throne may be made out, and in front, a figure apparently anointing him. Another holds a mirror, and at a green doorway are traces of a figure with a large oblong shield.

In the left chapel are only some traces of the painting that once adorned it; some cows, *aśoka* flowers, and parts of figures with considerable fragments of two long painted inscriptions and some smaller ones.

---

[1] Painting marked 'B' of 1874-75.

[2] Painting marked 'C' of 1874-75.

VII.—*The Ceiling.*

There is nothing left on the front wall. But the ceilings are the most complete in the whole series, and though blackened with smoke contain many very interesting pieces of floral decorations, Nâga Râjas, flying figures, others with human and animal heads, but the lower extremities ending in scroll-work. Several of these have been copied by Mr. Griffiths,[1] and are well deserving of publication.

VIII.

In the left end of the front aisle, on the right of the cell-door,[2] is a small scene. A tank or pond is represented with lotos (*kamala*) flowers and geese in it. On the brink of it sit a râja or other great man and his wife, and behind her to the right, hangs a long straight sword in its scabbard and a small shield with it. In the background are the conventional forms indicative of mountain scenery.

On the left side of the cell-door is more hill scenery, and over a hill on the left comes a man with a sword. To the right is another carrying two geese, and below, beside a pond, are two geese and two men standing in the water,—the one on the right having a sword hung by a strap over his left shoulder (exactly like the one carried by the man above, and that hung up in the first section of the picture), he is represented as lifting water in his right hand as if to perform the *sañkalapa*. The other, resembling the man carrying the geese (and probably the same), seems to have completed his *sañkalapa*, and just thrown the water away.

IX.

Above the cell-door the painting is much destroyed, but has apparently consisted of two parts. On the extreme left a large goose is represented on a seat, and to the right is a woman whose head-dress has a circular frill behind from which depend two quilled or puffed ends or 'banderoles.' Above is a green seated figure, and to the right sits another with his hands joined, while a third, in white clothing stands behind. The rest of the picture here is destroyed.

Between two pillars of a palace stands a man in white clothing resting on a long stick or bambu with a straight sword by his left side—he is probably a *chokidâr* or porter.

In the compartment to the right, a râja sits on either side, the one on the right with his feet on a low footstool (*pâda-pîṭha*), and beside it a dish with a water lily. He holds his hands in the *dharmachakra mudrâ* of Buddha as if giving instruction. Behind him is a blue pillow and the ornamented corner of the back of the seat. The râja on the left has a highly jewelled *mukuṭa* with other jewellery and holds up his left hand. Between them two men sit on a cushion who may be their diwâns, the one on the left holding his hand up as if in the act of speaking. Behind each prince is a *châmara*-bearer. In the extreme left of the picture sit two women, and in the hands of one of them the râja's sword. Beside the other sit two more figures.

X.

On the side of the pilaster to the right of this, are two women, one with a cloth across her bosom, a *pârkala* about her waist, and a flower or fruit in her

[1] Painting Nos. 8, 9, 10, 11 and 12 of 1874-75; No. 20, 21 of 1875-76; and Nos. 25, 26, 27, 28 and 29 to 35 of 1877-78.

[2] For the positions of these paintings, see Plate V.

left hand. The other is taller and has a fine armlet (*bahubandha*) and a waist-chain (*kaṭî, mekhalâ*, or *kanchî*). Her thighs are apparently cased in a net work of beads, perhaps the pattern of the fine muslin robe she wears.

XI.

On the front of the pilaster is a small painting which has been copied by Mr. Griffiths,[1] who remarks that "it is very dilapidated, but enough remains to show that the original was a very graceful composition. On the left is a man in a *dhôtî* sitting cross-legged on the floor, with the left forearm resting on the knee, examining something, perhaps a portion of his necklace, in his right hand. The pose of the woman on the right, who is entirely nude,[2] is admirable. From the action of her right hand she appears to be stretching a band, but from the action of the left it seems as if the material were rigid. What it is intended to represent I cannot make out."

XII.

Close to this, the lower compartment to the left of the door of the first cell in the aisle is too much destroyed to be intelligible. The figures seem to be mostly females, four are in front, and one has apparently been reaching across the centre of the picture. One above was, perhaps, playing a triangular shaped musical instrument. An oval white object in the upper part of the painting, I cannot make out satisfactorily.

Just above, in an interior, sits a man, perhaps a small râja, on a cushion, and a woman resting her left hand on the ground is talking to him. He is attended as usual by a *châmara*-bearer.

XIII.

Above the door is another interior, representing three apartments or divisions (*tibâri*) of a hall. In the middle is a râja, on a cushioned seat with a pillow behind him, over which is seen the corners of the back carved with *makaras*; behind the head is a nimbus (*bhâmaṇḍala*), and his feet rest on a low stool, while his hands are in the attitude of speaking (*dhârmachakra mudrâ*) In the side compartments are a fair *châmara*-bearer in the left, and a dark one in the right. In front of each sit two men—a fair one on the inner side and a darker on the outer, alike in both, and in the same positions, the darker with higher *mukuṭas* than the fairer ones, who may be their diwâns. The *Brihat Saṁhita* lays down rules for the relative proportions of the *mukuṭas* of Râjas, Yuvarâjas, Diwâns, &c.

To the right the plaster has been much damaged, apparently wilfully.

XIV.

In a palace above the last there is a scene in which most of the figures are tolerably entire, and which merits early copying.

On a chair sits a Râja with his feet down and crossed on a footstool, one hand on his knee, the other raised a little, and a *mukuṭa* on his head. On his left his Rânî sits in a similar position but presented more from the side. A woman at her side rests her elbow on her knee and looks towards the râja. Behind each a fairer figure attends as *châmara*-bearer—the left hand one with a *tilaka*, or caste mark on her forehead, and the other with a Persian-like cap and hold-

[1] Painting marked 'A.' of 1875-76.

[2] I doubt if any figure is entirely nude; though, as already remarked, the dress of the higher class ladies is almost perfectly transparent.—J. B.

ing some object with both his hands. Beside him is a woman with a vessel in her left hand. In front sits a man, like a labourer or ploughman with moustache, speaking to the râja, and beside him two others. Beyond the pillar a man stands with a rosary in his hand looking up to a tall woman beyond the next pillar and laughing. She is dressed like a Rânî in much jewellery. Beyond her, to the left, is a man in the dress usually given to porters, and who appears to speak with her.

XV.

Below and between the doors of two cells we have another scene :—

Near the centre stands a noble lady holding up some object in her right hand. Before her, to the left, is a white dressed Bhikshu (perhaps Asita) with a *chhatra* over his head, into whose hands she has given an infant (Buddha). At his left side is a râja with flat-topped crown who seems to listen to him with great delight. Behind is a *châmara*-bearer also intently listening. In the door, to the left, is a porter, and beyond it is another figure with a Bhikshu's head-dress, but he is not in white (like Asita). Behind him are a man and woman, and below two people speaking to one another.

To the right of the Rânî stands her *dâsî* leaning forward, and before her a boy or pigmy. Behind the *dâsî* again, to the right, sits a man with a very large head-dress and the young Buddha perhaps before him. This picture is full of life.

A large piece of painting below seems as if left unfinished, with the figures outlined in red. If varnished they might perhaps be made intelligible.

XVI.

Over the cell-door is a Bhikshû holding up a lotos flower towards four Buddhas and between the doors of the second and third cells are eleven lines of Buddhas, ten in a row, a hundred and ten in all—all seated on lotoses and in red clothing ;—the last line seems to have been of a different colour from the rest.

XVII.

On the back wall, between the left chapel and antechamber, a large Buddha has sat under an *Âmba* (mango) tree, with an Indra on his right and a Bodhisattva on his left. His feet rest on a white lotos ; a worshipper is below a little to the left. Across the top are seven Buddhas in various *mudrâs*, each on a lotos, the stalks being brought up from below. On each side the *Bodhi-druma* or sacred tree are two Buddhas, the one pair darker than the other and one of each pair in the same *mudrâ*. Below these, on each side, were two pairs more, now nearly obliterated. Below, on the right side, is a pale coloured Buddha seated cross-legged, his hands in the *dharmachakra mudrâ*, with two attendant *chaurî*-bearers. Below is a painted inscription in letters of about the 6th century.

Deyadharmoyaṁ Sâkya Bhiksho Bhadanta Bu[*ddha*] *guptasya yadatra pûnyam* [*tad bhavatu*] *sarvasatva*..........

XVIII.

The roof of the antechamber to the shrine is beautifully decorated. Mr. Griffiths justly remarks that "The design is freely and boldly painted, and when seen under the conditions in which it was intended to be seen, the effect is most pleasing. The general arrangement is that of concentric bands mostly filled with conventional ornament, with the exception of the outer and principal one which partakes more of a naturalistic treatment of birds, of the lotos, and other flowers. The four corners are nearly repetitions of one another." "The two birds, with the quaint crests of conventional scrolls, and tails of the same character are constantly met with, both carved and painted. The piece of fret is well drawn in the portion of panel at the end."

The walls are covered with small painted figures of Buddha. Among those on the right hand side of the shrine-door are fragments of a painted inscription.

XIX.

In the shrine: On the front wall, on the right hand side of the door, is a Bodhisattva in the dress of a râja, like the right hand Dwârapâlas at Elurâ, and with two male attendants.

On the left is Avalôkitêśvara with a jug in his left hand, and a deer skin over his left shoulder.

The side walls are covered with Buddhas, in three lines of four each, with attendants without *chauris*—and all with aureoles.

The roof which is 12 feet high is also painted.[1] Mr. Griffiths remarks that "as it is almost totally dark here, it is reasonable to infer that the original must have been executed by means of artificial light. On entering the sanctuary with a light, the effect produced is one of extreme richness, the floating figures in the spandrils standing out with startling effect. These figures are bringing their gifts of flowers to present to the gigantic Buddha below. The wreath of flowers is admirably painted and the band of black and white with its varied simple ornament is a most happy idea, giving additional value to the rest of the design. The eye would have been satiated by the amount of colour were it not for the relief it derived from the imposition of this band."

XX.

On the back wall of the cave, between the antechamber and right side chapel has been a large figure of Indra on a hill. On his left was a sword bearer, a yellow dwarf at his foot, and three other attendants on his left. On his right were a female and another figure. Above them is a female, apparently nearly nude, leaning to the left, and still above is the arm, &c., of another better covered. On the right side above are a *Gandharva* and *Apsarâ*, sailing in the air towards Indra's head.

XXI.

In the left back chapel on the left hand wall, along the top from left to right, are two pairs of women looking down from two windows upon the scene below. In the middle is a red man floating on clouds, and to the right a *Gandharva* and *Apsarâ* on the same.

Below are three compartments of a building. On the left side of the middle one, leaning against the dividing pillar, is a tall woman of a deep clayey colour, with jewelled head-dress, and rich striped loin-cloth or *sâḍî*, speaking to a red female on her left. Behind this one again is a third lady of like complexion with the first, holding up a child which wears stockings, and who seems to wish to go to the first. In front is a fourth proceeding to the right and looking back to the first lady.

In the door to right (*i.e.*, in the third compartment) is the porter, and in a door facing him is a bald Bhikshu with a cloth over his shoulders and another round

[1] Mr. Griffiths's copy, No. 13 of 1874-75.

his loins, and a white coloured *chêlâ* or disciple before him carrying a bag and begging from the porter. Before the first lady (in the left compartment) are three women and four children or dwarfs. The fair lady, to the left, holds jewellery in her hand, the second is dark, and the third red and holds a flower vessel.

The first boy has a vessel on his back held up by a string over his shoulder; the dark one in front holds a long dish, the fourth is white and has a dark sash passing over his shoulders and under and over his arms.

Behind all stands the porter in white clothes, with a finger of his left hand raised and the palm of the right held out, as if giving some explanation.

XXII.

On the right side of this chapel the same tall lady seems to re-appear in the left side of the central compartment, her right hand raised, and the left across the body. Behind her are four women in line—two of them beyond the pillar, and the front one—of a dark green complexion. The next two are fair; the third clasps the pillar; and the fourth is reddish, with a white *chôlî*—(probably she is a *kañchukinî*). In front of the green woman is another reddish one—*a kañchukinî*—her person covered, and holding up a box; and behind her is a boy or dwarf. Before the fourth woman is another dwarf female with a bag in her hand; and behind all, on the right, is a white-vested porter with a stick in his hand and with long pointed moustache.

On the left are a white and a green woman, and in front a red and a green pigmy female. In the hands of the latter, who looks back towards the lady, is a flower tray. To the left of these is a man dresssed in light coloured clothes, who is addressing them. Above, in the centre, two ladies and a boy look out at a window; to the right is a *Gandharva and Apsarâ;* and to the left a peaked roof.

XXIII.

The ceiling of this small chamber is painted with great taste. The general arrangement is similar to the central area in all the other roofs, consisting of bands between concentric circles inscribed in a square, Mr. Griffiths thus describes it[1]:—" The outermost band is composed of diamond shaped forms, filled in with grotesque heads. These forms are connected by jewelled bosses, from which radiate floriated work. The next band is filled in with conventional foliage most beautifully and delicately drawn, golden in tone, on a black ground. Then we have a band with a procession of geese *(hañsa)*, the interspaces filled in with different coloured flowers, also on a black ground. If this band is carefully examined all round, it will be seen how pleasingly the space has been filled, how varied is the action of each bird, and how well has been rendered the peculiar characteristic movements of the goose. This band alone will give a fair notion of the amount of observation required before a result so admirable could have been attained. In the centre of the design was a rosette, the idea taken from the lotos.

" Taking the corners of the square diagonally, we find the triangular spaces of two filled with grotesque heads with grinning faces, large tusks and twisted horns" (*kîrtîmukhas*). " On either side of each head is floriated work, springing from other grotesque heads, which are well worthy of study. The ornament of the third triangular space is composed of a human-bodied creature, struggling with

[1] No. 23, Report for 1877-78.

a dragon, both of which terminate in floriated work. The colour and drawing have considerably faded in this example.

"The ornament filling the fourth space is admirably designed and drawn, consisting of a dragon, attacked by another mythological animal. The bodies of both are partly covered by scales and they terminate in floriated work, very similar to the conventional foliage, employed to represent the mantling in heraldry during the middle ages."

XXIV.

In the corresponding chapel to the right of the shrine, are two painted scenes, in which the principal figures are represented in the same light, red ochrey tints on a dark ground, as those in the chapel just described: perhaps they are of later date than the other paintings. On the left side are five female figures among hills; the first, on the left, in very thin dress, stands just before a plantain tree; the second and third have curious circular head-dresses, like that of the lady sculptured on the adjoining back wall of the room. The first has a bag, the second a casket, perhaps containing relics, and at their feet sit four small figures like boys, but with the head-dresses of females. The third lady has some small object in her left hand. The fourth wears a *mukuṭa* or crown, and leads by the hand a child carrying a stick, whilst a bigger one follows. Above the picture, on the left, are two *Arhats* in the clouds with their hands joined; in the centre is a conventional cave; and on the right are two flying figures.

XXV.

The right side of the room is painted in the same style. A Râja, on the left, sits on a circular mat, and a tall *châmara*-bearer with a round head-dress stands on his left. From the right two ladies approach him, naked to the waists, the last bearing a flower-tray, and behind her is a plantain tree. Between the *châmara*-bearer and these is a man carrying a bow and hastening towards the râja, while he looks round and speaks to the woman. Below stands another *châmara*-bearer, also a woman, and beside her are three children, one carrying some large object. On the left, below the râja, are three men (or boys), one bearing a cock or other bird.

Above, on the right, are parts of two figures in the clouds, one with a flower; and on the left a fat figure looking towards the sculpture on the back wall—of the infant Buddha on Gautamî's knee and Suddhodana.

XXVI.

The ceiling of this small room, like its neighbour in the other chapel, is also very fine. Mr. Griffiths says [1]: "It is an admirable specimen of ornamental design, and I would draw special attention to the four spandrils, each differently designed with a monster terminating in floriated scrolls, a treatment characteristic also of Roman, Mediæval, and Renaissance Art.

"The Buddhists' love of variety, as exemplified in these spandrils, affords a good lesson to a modern ornamentist, who would be satisfied with designing one, spandril only, and filling up the rest by stencilling, or some other mechanical means."

"Were there nothing left of the paintings, but these two small ceilings in Cave No. 2, they would be enough to attest the very high state to which de-

[1] *Report* for 1875-76, p. 9., No. 22.

corative art, both in design and execution, had attained during the age of Buddhism."

XXVII.

To the right of the back pilaster, in the right side aisle of the hall, is a spotted deer standing on the edge of a conventionalized river; and again in the river is a man hanging over the back of the deer who is carrying him across.

Above this the painting is too much defaced to be made out, except that another deer appears.

XXVIII.

The remainder of this wall bears one of the most interesting groups of pictures now left in the caves, which it is to be regretted we have not yet a copy of, for the bats are fast ruining it.[1] It seems to be all one subject and might be painted entire, except, perhaps, the two lower portions.

Between the second and third cell-doors below is the retinue of a rajâ. He goes out on a large elephant, with the umbrella of state over his head, and the *ankuśa* or goad in his hand; behind him is an attendant with the *châmara*; at his side goes a smaller elephant, with a rider now defaced; and before it walks a man with some load in a bag on his back. In front (to the left) five horses (two of them green) advance,—the men on the green horses looking back to the râja. There are also fourteen men on foot, of whom eleven seem to be soldiers, some carrying oblong shields, and three round ones with a great grinning Gorgon face painted on the front of each. Two above on the extreme left have swords in scabbards; nine others have Nêpal *khukhaḍîs* or *dabiyas*, but very long; other two men play flutes; and one beats a drum (*ḍaka*).

XXIX.

Between the first and second cell-doors, below, is represented, with a conventionalism worthy of the Chinese, a river (perhaps the Gangâ) with many fish and shells in it. A boat with three masts, a jib sail, and an oar behind, and filled towards the stern with ten *matkas* or earthenware jars,—carries a man in it with long hair, who is praying (Plate VII, fig. 1). In the heaven behind, Chandra—the Moon, a figure with a crescent behind him, is represented as coming to him, followed by another figure. A Nâga Râja and his wife in the water seem to draw the boat back; and below is represented another similar figure with a human head and long tail in the water. On the left, to which the boat is going, is Buddha on the shore, and a figure worshipping him. On the shores rocks are conventionally painted.

XXX.

Above the third cell-door a lady looks out of a balcony towards the right.[2] Above the sowars (in No. 28), to the left, a râja and a man on each side of him sit on a couch talking, and two others sit below,—one of them apparently explaining something to the râja before whom he sits. Behind the râja stand two women, one with a *châmara*, and a third on the extreme left stands behind the seated man. In a balcony, to the right, two ladies sit talk-

---

[1] Why are they not shut out as Mr. Griffiths suggested?

[2] This and the other groups, all along the upper part of the wall, are so much darker in general tint than those in the middle and below, that one might be inclined to believe they belonged to different stories, if not to different dates.

ing, and in the court below is a horse; also on the roof of the balcony is another horse. The horse seems to be a connecting link among these pictures and appears six times. In a palace, again to the right and on the left side of the central cell-door, a râja sits on a cushioned seat holding a flower in his right hand. Behind him stand four ladies, one holding a flower in her hand, and all with deep bracelets, *saḍîs*, and rich jewellery. On the râja's left a man sits below, and in front (to the left) is another man with a fillet and necklace; while a third comes in dressed in blue blouse and Persian head-dress, and apparently addresses the râja,—perhaps respecting the horse outside.

Above the first described part of this, a râja or great man and perhaps his diwân, are represented as sitting talking together. Before them sits another man apparently addressing them. Two women are seated in front, and at the râja's left the back of one is turned to the spectator showing well how her hair is dressed. Behind the râja are two women standing, one with a *châmara*, and inside the door, to the left, another stands looking at the scene.

Behind the man who sits before the two principal personages, stands another with fillet, jewelled necklaces, and a scanty blue cloth about his loins, and just behind him is the horse on the roof of the balcony already mentioned.

Above this sit two men on the grass, or a green carpet, and before them is a long board with a line down the middle of it and divided into twelve squares across —twenty-four in all. Again to the right of it some great man sits with another beyond him. Right in front a woman is seated, looking towards the first of these two.

A space of about a foot wide with rock in it, over a horse facing the next, divides this from the following palace scene. In it some important personage sits on a low seat and another on his right on a cushion, covered with chintz. To their right sits a Nâga Râja and speaks to the one on the seat, while the other listens. Two women also sit behind the Nâga Râja and listen. To the right and a little above, in a balcony, are two women and a boy, and in a window below a man and woman are seated. To the right of this is a door, in front of which is a horse ridden by a man, and beyond it are steps up to the palace; up which the man is also represented as having ridden.

Below the stair again and to the right, is a shed and a lady swinging herself in it while another (or the same) leans against a pillar of the shed and speaks to a man or woman who leads a horse towards her from the left; the horse being at the upper right hand side of the second cell-door. A little to the right of the lady in the swing, on some raised place sit a Nâga Râja with five snake hoods and his diwân with three. The râja stretches his right hand towards four ladies, who address him from the left, while the diwân inclines his head towards them as if pleased.

Above the swing and extending to the roof of the cave is a scene in which sits a Nâga Râja to the right and his Nâganî on his right; a woman stands behind each. Two men sit before the râja on the left, one of them on a seat; and to the right is a Nâganî, and a Nâga man with two *phaṇas* or hoods over his head.

Outside, to the right, sit other two men—just over the other Nâga Râja and his diwân. All these attendants sit in a circle round the central Nâga Râja and his wife.

XXXI.

To the right of the last are two *Śishyas* or disciples following a Bhikshu. Above are two *arhats* or holy men, flying in the air. A man approaches to worship the Bhikshu with a water-pot (*gharâ*) in his hand. Behind him are two others bearing flower trays, and with them stand three women, all paying reverence to the Bhikshu. To the right of this and between it and the pilaster a building is represented.

XXXII.

Below the Bhikshu in the last, and to the right of the Nâga Râja and his diwân in the one before, are two women with five musicians, one playing on large cymbals *(jhañja)*, one on the conch (*śankha*), one blowing a long straight trumpet (*turî* or *bhungalâ*), one beating a drum (*mṛidañga*) suspended by a cord over his shoulders, and it is not clear what the fifth, who has a moustache, plays upon. Another man in blue and white *dhôtî* stands before the first two women.

XXXIII.

Under the preceding scenes and extending from the first to the second cell-door is a series of pictures just over the ship (No. 29), which seem to be intended as representations of what went on outside the palace walls, while what has been depicted above are laid within.

Under the Nâga Râja and his diwân (in No. 30) is the great door of a palace in which two women are represented, the one on the right, wearing a petti-coat striped blue and black, and holding a bason in her hands at which the other looks.

To the left of the door, and a little lower, a great man and his companions advance towards it,—his left hand laid on that of his attendant. The first, near the door, looks back and carries an oblong shield and the usual blue sword, like a large Nepalese *khukhaḍî*. Two follow close behind him, one also looking back towards the big man. Beyond these stands another, also looking towards him. Then comes the principal personage and an attendant on either side, while in front is a servant with blue loin-cloth carrying a loaded tray. Behind follow two women, one with a striped petticoat, the other with a double fillet or snood in her hair. And in the compartments of a balcony above sit three figures, perhaps musicians.

To the left, in a house, two women, one at least of high grade, sit talking, while from within a lady comes with a heaped bason and in front of her another decends the steps which are just at the heels of the great man's retinue above described.

To the right side of the palace door (and at the edge of the door of the first cell) is another house in which is seen a *Bhikshu* on a seat. To his left sits another, perhaps his *śishya*. Before the first, and to the left, are seven men, and in the foreground two women, all seated with their hands clasped. The second man is distinguished by a fillet in his hair and he and another sit on blue cushions, the rest on the ground. The Bhikshu is giving them a sermon (*upadeśa*), to which all listen attentively.

On the right of the first cell-door sits a great man and his wife, and two women stand behind them, one with a *châmara*.

XXXIV.

On the front of the pilaster has been a tall male figure with bare legs, a female on his left, and a fat dwarf on his right.

XXXV.

On the end of the front aisle, in the upper left corner, a râja sits in his palace, holding a naked straight sword across in front of him. At his left kneels a *kânî* and her *dâsî*, the former with rich waistbelt (*mekhalâ*), &c. The *dâsî* leans her head against her hand as if in sorrow, the elbow resting on her knee. Before the râja—to the right, and similarly dressed "in Coan vesture," another kneeling rânî lays her hands on his feet, and touches the ground with her head as if earnestly pressing some request. Beyond her, a red-skinned lady raises her hands to her face as if saluting, asking pardon, or beseeching favour, and to the right a man in white-and-blue striped kirtle goes out of the palace.

Outside a tall man stands with a rod or spear in his hand and in striped waistcloth. Behind him sits a woman in green clothing, and in the back ground is another standing figure. The rest of the picture to the right is destroyed.

Below, on the left side, has been another palace scene. In it a râja is seated with his feet on a footstool. On his right sits a female in *chôlî* and rich head-dress, and behind him another of reddish complexion plying a square mat fan, seen to the right of his head as if bent round by the action. On his left a *kañchukinî* enters in white *chôlî*, while another figure stood in front, but is destroyed.

Behind the râja is a shaven-headed, fair-skinned old Brahman or Bhikshu in light pale green clothes. Behind him a female in blue-and-white striped petticoat, leans against the pillar; and in the foreground sit the *rânî* and *dâsî*—apparently the same who appear to the left above.

XXXVI.

On the extreme right (at the edge of the cell-door) is a richly dressed half nude lady holding up a chaced vessel hung by three chains. In front of her appears the head of another; below can be traced an elephant and two men beyond it; a human figure in a recess; and the heads of a red and a green horse.

XXXVII.

To the right of the door sits a râja on a couch with his feet on a stool and his hands in the attitude of instructing. Behind him, a woman holds a *châmara*; to his right a pale figure with peaked Persian cap, jewels in the ears, and full clothing, holds a dish in the left hand; and behind is a yellow woman with a *châmara*. Below this, and in front of the râja two yellow-skinned men are seated wearing *dupatta* (*S. Uttarîya*) and *dhôtî*, but with crowns, and rings on their arms and wrists, though without pearls or other jewels. They seem to address the râja, while between them and him sits an ill-drawn pink figure apparently interpreting. Below is a seated female servant.

Under this there seem to have been elephants.

XXXVIII.

On the return of the front wall is a tall male figure, with a female on his left and two males on his right, among mountain scenery.

CAVE III.

This is a small vihâra higher up on the face of the rock, but quite unfinished. The verandah is 29 feet by 7, and supported by four pillars and two pilasters, only blocked out. An entrance has been made for the hall, but little of it has been excavated. There is also a commencement of an under-storey to this cave.

CAVE IV.

We now come to Cave IV. (Fergusson's No. 3), the largest *Vihâra* of the series. The verandah is about 87 feet long, 11¾ wide, and 16 feet high, supported by eight octagonal columns with plain bracket capitals. There is a room 10 feet by 8½ at each end, entered by a small door with three steps. The cave has had a façade outside, carved with *chaitya*-window ornaments containing figures of Buddha.

The windows are surrounded by neat tracery with a female and attendant at the bottom of each jamb. The hall is entered by one central and two side doors, and has two windows between the doors. The large door, though considerably damaged, to about 2 feet above the floor, to which depth the cave was long filled with earth, is one of the most elaborate to be found here; generally it resembles that of Cave II, but no mere description could do justice to its details. The *dwârapâlas* were females attended by dwarfs. The upper compartment of the architrave on the right contains a bull, lying much as the Nandi does before Śaiva temples; and on the upper member of the cornice, at the extreme right, two monkeys are carved. The frieze is ornamented by five models of the chaitya-window, three containing Buddhas, and the end ones, pairs of human figures. At the upper corners of the door are figures somewhat like goats rampant (*śârdûlas*) facing each other, and which have had riders, but they are broken. To the right of the door, and between it and the architrave of the window, there is a large compartment sculptured with a variety of figures at the side, and in the middle a large one of Padmapâni, the Bôdhisatva of Amitâbha, the fourth *Dnyânî* or divine Buddha, and who is supposed to be incarnate in the Dalai Lama of Lhasa; the arms are both broken, but the figure of Amitâbha Buddha is on his forehead. The head is surrounded by a nimbus, and the remains of the lotos may be traced on his left hand. The compartments, four on each side, represent the Bauddha Litany. This may be regarded as an evidence of the later age of this cave approaching to those of the Ḍheḍwâḍâ at Elurâ and Cave VII. at Aurangâbâd.[1] There are also pieces of sculpture very similar to this behind, one of the Dahgobas in the vihâra to the right of the chaitya, and in some of the smaller caves at Kaṇhêri, and two versions outside the façade of Cave XXVI. here, as well as a painted one in Cave XVII. Above this is a small horse-shoe shaped compartment with a Buddha sitting inside.

There is no painting in the cave, except traces of a small fragment in very brilliant colours on the roof of the verandah to the right of the central door. Portions of the roof inside appear as if a layer of the rock had fallen off near the front, and the workmen had begun to smooth it again from the back. It was, however, never finished.

The antechamber is 21 feet by 13. On each side the shrine-door is a large standing Buddha, and on each end wall of the antechamber are two similar figures; but, with the shrine and cells, it is much infested with bats. The Buddha in the shrine is in the usual *dharmachakra-mudrâ*,—the left hand attend-

1 See *Archæological Survey of Western India*, vol. III.

ant holding a lotos in his left hand. The wheel and deer are in front, and quite a group of worshippers at each corner of the throne. The hall is 87 feet square, and is supported by twenty-eight columns, 3 feet 2 inches to 3 feet 3 inches in diameter, of the same style as in the verandah, plain, and without the elaborate tracery in Caves I and II, but with a deep architrave over them, as at Ghatoṭkach, which raises the roof of the cave considerably. The front aisle is 97 feet in length and has a cell at each end.

We descend to the next by a rough rocky path.

CAVE V.

Cave V. is only the commencement of a *vihâra*, the verandah of which is 45½ feet by 8 feet 8 inches; but of the four pillars, only one is nearly finished, and it is of the same style as those of the last cave, only shorter and with a square base. The door has an architrave round it, divided into six compartments on each side, and each filled by a pair of standing figures in various attitudes. In the lintel are nine divisions, the central one with Buddha and attendants and the others with pairs of seated figures. Two very neat colonettes support the frieze in which are five *chaitya*-window ornaments. Outside is a roll-pattern member and a border of leaves; but at the upper corners these are carried outwards so as to surround a female standing on a *makara* under foliage of the Aśoka and Mango, and attended by a small dwarf.

The left window is also richly carved, but scarcely any progress has been made inside.

CAVE VI.

This cave is of two-storeys. From the lower, the whole of the verandah has fallen away. The outer wall is panelled under the four large windows which light a hall, 53 feet 4 inches wide and 54 feet 10 inches deep—the front and back aisles being about 71 feet long, with chambers at the ends of each 8 feet by 10. Having been occupied by natives who used to light their fires in it, this cave is much ruined, and has a very dilapidated appearance. The columns are arranged in four rows of four each—sixteen in all—but only seven are now standing with four thin pilasters in the lines of the rows on each wall. Five columns have fallen within the last forty years. Between the pilasters are three chambers on each side, each fully 8 feet by 9, and all with niches in their back walls. The pillars are about 13 feet high, plain octagons to about three-fourths of their height, above which they are sixteen-sided, without bases, and having a cincture under a sixteen-sided fillet at the top; imitation beams only 2 or 3 inches deep run from one pillar to another. The columns in front of the antichamber are somewhat similar in character to those in the porticos of Cave VII. The antichamber is 13 feet 4 inches deep, and the sanctuary is 10 feet by 15½. The figure of Buddha, which has apparently been painted blue, is seated in the *dharmachakra-mudrâ*, on a pedestal 3 feet high, with wheel and small deer in front and supported at the corners by lions: the usual attendants are wanting. It is quite separate from the back wall, along the upper part of which is a recess. The door to the sanctuary is slightly arched with *makara toraṇas* at the spring of the arch, and a *Nâga* figure with two attendants under the centre of it.

The stair in the front aisle, leading to the upper-storey, has been broken away below. It lands in the verandah above. This verandah has been supported by four columns and two pilasters; but only one of the latter now remains, which is a particularly fine one. Above the stair landing are many small Buddhas carved on the walls and two Dahgobas. Outside the vernadah there are small chapels with sculptured Buddhas. There are also at each end of the verandah open chambers with carved pillars, and inside these chambers there are rooms, 11 feet by 9. The hall is 53 feet wide by 50 feet deep and 11¼ high, supported by twelve plain columns, enclosing the usual square area. The pillars have square bases and octagonal shafts, changing to square under the bracket capitals, which are sculptured with figures of Buddha in small recesses. Opposite the central inter-space of each side, and at the end of the left aisle are chambers or chapels with pillars in front, each leading to an inner cell. There are also three cells on each side, and one at the end of the right aisle. Over the chapel in the left end of the front aisle, the frieze is carved with elephants, spiritedly cut,—one of them killing a tiger. A portion of the right side aisle has never been cleared out to the level of the floor.

The antechamber is 16 feet by 8⅓. The plain octagon pillars in front of it have each a *śârdûla* bracket. This room has a tall standing Buddha, carved in recesses, on each side the shrine-door, which may have been added after the cave was finished, but not probably. On the right end are two such figures with a group of worshippers between; and on the left side is one tall Buddha and three smaller standing and three squatting ones, all in recesses.

This cave has more sculptured figures of Buddha than any other vihâra here and many standings ones. On the back wall to the left of the antechamber is another standing Buddha, and over the left chapel seven small seated ones and one squatting. The chapel on this side is empty. On the upper part of the left side wall are fourteen Buddhas, mostly seated, and outlines of three Daghobas. In recesses of the front wall are nine Buddhas of various sizes, mostly on *padmâsanas* supported by *Nâgas*; and along the wall head, in the right aisle, are sixteen squatting Buddhas. The shrine contains the usual statue of Buddha squatting in the *dharmachakra mudrâ* on a *siñhâsana*. The lions, deer, and wheel are in bas-relief. The usual attendants stand on each side of Buddha; and five tall standing Buddhas on each side wall; also two smaller ones above one another on each side of the door.

On the back wall, to the right of the shrine, are one large and two smaller Buddhas, and thirteen squat ones above.

In the right chapel is a squat Buddha on a *siñhâsana*, attended by two Bodhisatvas, with a *Vidyâdhara* and *Apsarâ* above on each side. On the right wall is another seated Buddha and attendant, unfinished; on the left are two standing Buddhas of different heights. The chapel in the right end of the front aisle contains the usual image and attendants and has over its front three small Buddhas and five Dahgobas.

This is perhaps one of the most recent caves in the series.

The Paintings in Cave VI.

The few fragments of painting on the back wall of the lower storey, and in the antechamber are so smoked that nothing can be made out of them, except that a large palace scene was on the left back wall, and Indra-like figures on both sides of the shrine-door.

The upper-storey has been painted, but it has almost entirely disappeared. The front of the chapel in the right end of the front aisle still retains fragments of the painting; and inside, the walls have been covered with painted Buddhas. In the left chapel in front, on each side the cell-door, is a painted Dravidian building—a *Vihâra*—on the inside of the verandah roof of which is a circular ornament, with strings of pearls hanging from it, and inside the vihâra has been a seated Buddha.

On the side walls, the fragments have been scribbled over by natives and are scarcely traceable.

Those on the outside of the front wall of the cave are in even worse condition. The pattern can be made out on parts of the ceiling.

CAVE VII.

Cave VII. is a Vihâra somewhat differing in type from any yet described. In front of the verandah were two porches, each supported by two advanced octagonal pillars with capitals somewhat like those in Cave II. and at Elephanta. The frieze above is ornamented with the favourite Chaitya-window device. The verandah measures 62 feet 10 inches long by 13 feet 7 inches wide and 13 feet 6 inches high. There is no hall, but in the back wall are four cells, and the antechamber leading to the shrine; and at each end of the verandah are rooms at some height above the floor with two pillars in front, each again opening into three cells, about 8½ feet square. The shrine in an unequal four-sided room, in which Buddha is seated at the back on a low *Siñhâsana* or lion-throne, having in front of the seat two lions at the ends, and two antelopes facing each other with a small wheel or *chakra* between them. His legs are crossed under him, his right hand raised in the *aśiva mudrâ* or attitude of blessing, and the left holding his robe, and with high *mukuṭa*. From behind Buddha a *makara's* head projects on each side; there is a figured halo behind his head; and much carving round about him; a male *chauri*-bearer stands on either side behind the *makara's* head; and in the corners, above their heads are *Gandharvas*, *Vidyâdharas*, or Buddhist cherubs. The projection of the *siñhâsana* is carried round the sides, and carved in front with eight squatting Buddhas on each side. Upon this projection stand three Buddhas on each side, also with aureoles behind their heads, those next the central Buddha are of smaller stature, but the other two are gigantic figures—each holds his left hand up to his breast, with the edge of his robe in it, whilst the right hangs by his side with the palm turned out. Between these figures are other small cross-legged ones. The sides of the antechamber are entirely covered with small Buddhas sculptured in rows of five to seven each, sitting or standing on lotoses and with lotos leaves between them. The stalk of the lowest central lotos is upheld by two kneeling figures with regal head-dresses canopied by the many headed *nâga* behind each; on the left is a kneeling figure and two standing Buddhas, and on the right a Buddha is behind the *Nâga*, and behind him are three worshippers with presents. The door into the sanctuary has four standing and three sitting Buddhas on each side, carved in alternate compartments of the architrave, and eight sitting ones above; at the foot of the architrave is a lion's head and paws. The pilasters outside the architrave are supported by dwarfs, and divided into three compartments, containing a standing Buddha in the lower and cross-legged ones in the compartments above, whilst over the capitals a female figure stands under foliage and on a *makara*.

Outside this, the wall is divided into three nearly square compartments, each ornamented with small pilasters at the sides, and all, except the two upper ones on the right, having *gandharvas* in the corners over the large cross-legged Buddhas which occupy them; these have all 'glories' behind their curly-haired heads, except the upper one on the right, which has the protection of the snake with seven hoods.

The Paintings in Cave VII.

In Cave VII there is a piece of painting on the backwall, left side, rather faint, but, if varnished, it might come out. A Buddha is represented on an *âsana*; on the right side a woman sits, on the left a woman with white *sâḍî* and purple *dhôtî*, another with striped clothing, and behind some other figures. Over the door, to the right, can be traced the feet of a *gandharva*.

On the right side is a still larger piece, in which the outlines of figures in buildings are traceable. On the ceiling are also parts of the pattern.

CAVE VIII.

Cave VIII, on the east side of the last, is a Vihâra cave which has lost the whole of its front. What remains of its hall is 32 feet 4 inches long by about 17 feet deep and 10 feet high. It is the lowest down in the rock, and was formerly choked up with earth. There are two cells in each end, and two on each side of the antechamber to the shrine. This latter is entered by a low door, and contains only a low stone bench at the back, but no trace of an image.

CAVE IX.

Cave IX is a small Chaitya or Temple Cave of a very early age, probably dating from the first century B. C. It is 45 feet deep by 22 feet 9 inches wide and 23 feet 2 inches high. A colonnade all round divides the nave from the aisles, and at the back the pillars form a semicircular apse, in the center of which stands the *Chaitya* or Dahgoba, about 7 feet in diameter; its base is a plain cylinder, 5 feet high, supporting a dome 4 feet high by about 6 feet 4 inches in diameter, surmounted by a square capital, about 1¼ feet high, and carved on the sides in imitation of the "Buddhist railing." It represents a relic box, and is crowned by a projecting lid—a sort of abacus consisting of six plain fillets, each projecting over the one below. This supported a wooden umbrella as at Kârlê. Besides the two pillars inside the entrance, which are square below and above but octagonal in the middle, the nave has twenty-one plain octagonal columns without base or capital, 10 feet 4 inches high, supporting an entablature, 6 feet 8 inches deep, from which the vaulted roof springs, and which has originally been fitted with wooden ribs. The aisles are flat-roofed, and only an inch higher than the columns. These aisles are lighted by a window opening into each. Over the front aisle is the great window—one of the peculiar features of a Chaitya-cave; it is of horse-shoe form, about 11½ feet high, with an inner arch, about 9¾ feet high, just over the front pillars of the nave; outside this is the larger one with horizontal ribs, of which five on each side project in the direction of the centre, and eleven above in a vertical direction. On the sill of this arch is a terrace, 2¼ feet wide, with a low parapet in front, wrought in the "Buddhist-rail" pattern; outside this again, is another terrace over the porch, about 3¾ feet wide, and extending the whole width of the cave—the front of it being ornamented with patterns of the window itself as it must have originally appeared—with a wooden lattice-work in the arch. At each end of this, on the wall at right angles to the façade, is sculptured a large figure of Buddha, and on the projecting rock on each side there is a good deal of sculpture, but all of a much later date than the temple itself, and possibly of the fifth century. The porch of the door has partly fallen away. It seems to have had a cornice above, supported by two very wooden-like struts, similar to those in the Bhâjâ Chaitya.

The Paintings in Cave IX.

But little of the painting remains in this cave; but, as already noted, it is of two or even three periods. On different parts of the walls two layers of painting can be distinctly traced. The fragments copied by Mr. Griffiths,[1] and which he supposes belong to the earliest portions of the decoration of this cave, do appear to be older than what we find elsewhere, but they are certainly of more recent date than the fragment to be first described, which is still pretty entire and in which the dresses, heavy jewellery, earrings, necklaces, bracelets and head-dresses all remind us most vividly of the style of the Sânchi and Amrâvati topes, and of the earliest sculptures discovered at Mathurâ, and quite different from anything else left in these caves, except the fragments in Cave X., whence we may infer that it must belong to a period not later than the time say of Gautamîputra II. in the latter half of the second century.

I.

Over the left or west window of the cave on the inside of the front wall is this early piece of painting, possibly a version of the *jâtaka* of Śibi Râja, of which we shall meet a later representation in Cave XVII.

In this, a râja is representated sitting with one foot on the ground and the other on the seat, wearing a broad heavy neck-chain with large oblong jewels or clasps slipped over it, large earrings, and a sort of high turban with a knob in front, such as is seen on the heads of the men in the capitals of the columns at Kârlê and Bêḍsâ and in the sculptures on the Chaitya at Nâsik and Vihâra of Gautamîputra I. On his wrist are four massive rings, and on his arm a large bracelet. Two men stand behind him, one on either side, and four more with a woman before him. In the back-ground, to the left, two men come in with the high turbans already noticed, one of them with very large oblong earring, both with broad, sash-like, necklaces run through oblong jewels or discs, and heavy chased bracelets on their wrists, and with long narrow *dhôtîs*. Above is a flying figure similarly dressed, and perhaps intended for Indra. Over the lintel of the window are the heads of two Buddhas, also of later date, and partly covering the lower edge of the picture above.

To the left of this, on a hill, two men sit under an *Aśoka* tree. Over the door the painting is of a more recent date.

II.

Proceeding along the left wall from the front, the lower portions are totally pealed off: above are six Buddhas with three umbrellas each (*tribhuvanadhipatya*). Along the rest of the wall beyond these, the plaster is too much

[1] *Report for* 1874-75, pages 6 to 8, paintings 'A,' 'B.' 'C.' and 'D.'

smoked to make anything out except some traces of buildings and among them a short of temple.

Below, the wall has been painted in a later style with Buddhas.

The roof has been divided into a double row of squares with a rosette painted in each. On the pillars are figures of Buddha sitting and standing, and of the Dahgoba.

III.

On the back wall is a large scene, copied in four sections by Mr. Griffiths, who remarks that they "are all that remain of the decoration of the end wall, which is much to be regretted : for, beside their high artistic merit, they illustrate some of the ceremonials of the religious life of Buddhism."

On the extreme left Buddha sits on a hill and two disciples before him, while a third figure stands in the back ground.[1] At his right side is a bottle (for perfume ?) and below a figure (partly destroyed) bends forward, pouring something from a bottle into a small vessel. To the right, near a palace Buddha stands with his *bhikshupâtra* or alms-bowl, facing the left, and three beggars (one with beard and *jaṭâ* head-dress) and a young Bhikshu before him. Behind them, a bottle or jug with narrow neck is hung up in a sort of tripod. A man on a ladder ascending to the upper floor or roof of the palace receives a *kumbha* or pitcher from the shoulders of another to the left and a third is ascending the ladder to the right of the latter, also with a pitcher.

To the right of this stands a tall *Bodhisattva* with his right hand raised, and holding a bottle in his left with a *jaṭâ* head-dress, a deer skin over his left shoulder, and a white *dhôtî* round his loins held up by a green ribbon. To the right above is a white object not made out.

To the right of this[2] again is a figure of Buddha seated on a rich throne with his feet on a lotos flower in the teaching (*dharmachakra mudrâ*) attitude, and below the throne a square on which was an inscription of which only "*ya dharma*" can now be read. Two richly jewelled attendants behind the throne hold *châmaras*, and in the foreground, on Buddha's right, is a figure in *jaṭâ* head-dress and striped robe, holding a vessel in which there appear to be flowers, while a garland of them hangs from his finger.

Below sit a râja with square crown and his rânî—very pale (probably the colour has faded). On Buddha's proper left a Bhikshu with acquiline nose in *jaṭâ* head-dress approaches with a garland or *Mâlâ* between his hands, making a salâm. In front sit some man of note and his lady "extremely well drawn, in a very graceful attitude ;"—the man with a musical instrument in his lap, the end of which projects up in front of Buddha's robe ; and closer to Buddha and more in the foreground, is seen the head and shoulders of a disciple looking up at Buddha. This side of the picture seems to be intended to represent part of the scene as in a cave.

Still to the right, is a *Chaitya* or *Dahgoba* with three umbrellas over it, and on the left of it a man in the dress of a *sâdhu* holds his ears as he seems fervently to cry to it. On the base of it is a line of inscription.

---

[1] On Mr. Griffiths's first section 'A'.

[2] Mr. Griffiths's second section, 'B.' begins here.

To the right is Buddha[1] standing on a lotos with the nimbus round his head and an umbrella hung with strings of pearls, his right hand is held down before him and the palm turned up, while with the left he holds his robe. At his foot is a small Bhikshu, and behind, a part of the striped dress of the umbrella-holder is seen. In the next compartment Buddha sits on a throne with the nimbus round his head, his feet on a lotos, the stalk of it held by two small Nâga figures with snake tails. Below this was an inscription of which only "*(para) mopâsaka*" can now be made out.

Two richly-dressed figures stand beside Buddha, (one on his left with the *vajra*) holding *châmaras*. On the left sit a râja with high square-topped crown and perhaps his rânî. Above them a *Kinnara* sits on, or flies over, a ledge and points to Buddha. Just before the râja is a disciple or boy making *namaskâra* with the closed palms.

On the right a *Bhikshu* and his *Śishya*, or perhaps two disciples kneel and pay respect. Farther to the right other two figures, richly dressed, are destroyed.

About a foot broad of the painting to the right of this is totally destroyed, and then comes another fragment.

On the left[2] is a sitting Buddha, his feet on a stool, teaching, and below it an inscription of which "*ddha*" and "*saka*" only are legible. To the right is a fair standing figure, with jewellery, thin scarf, and *dhôtî*, holding a *châmara*; and three small figures sit before Buddha, making presents. To the left is a tall standing Buddha, and two little *Bhikshus* sit before him, towards whose heads he stretches his right hand. "The graceful attitude of the standing figure of Buddha," Mr. Griffiths remarks, "requires no comment. With the right hand extended, upon the palm of which can be traced the emblem of the wheel, with the left supporting a portion of the robe, an ornamental nimbus behind the head, and standing on the lotos, he is receiving or addressing two children who have come with their offerings to pay him homage. On the right, beside Buddha, is a fragment of a figure, which I believe to be another *chaurî*-bearer. On the right of this, again, a little to the foreground is another fragment of a child which balances the composition by tallying with the one on the extreme left. Over the two figures of Buddha can just be traced portions of the ennobling *chhatrîs*."

Scarcely a trace of painting now remains on the right wall.

IV.

On the triforium to the right of the Dahgoba is a large piece, but until it is varnished, nothing can be made out except umbrellas and some tall figures.

Further forward are more yellow Buddhas sitting and standing with attendants and under *chhatrîs*.

V.

On the front wall, to the right side of the door, the old painting has been covered by a later coating, which has partly peeled off, but so as to leave neither the earlier nor the later picture intelligible.

---

[1] This is the third section 'C,' of Mr. Griffiths's copies.

[2] This is on the fourth Section 'D' of Mr. Griffiths's copies from this wall.

CAVE X.

The oldest Chaitya-cave is No. X. Like the Bhâjâ one, it most possibly had at first a wooden front, now entirely gone, and later probably the lower half was of brick. The cave measures 41 feet 1 inch wide, about 95½ feet deep, and 36 feet high. The inner end of the cave, as well as of the colonnade that surrounds the nave, is semicircular, the number of columns in the latter being thirty-nine plain octagons—two more than in the great Chaitya at Kârlê, but many of them are broken. They are 14 feet high, and over them rises a plain entablature, 9½ feet deep, from which springs the arched roof, rising 12½ feet more, with a span of about 23½ feet. Like Bhâjâ, Kârlê, Bêḍsâ, Kondânê, &c., it has been ribbed with wood. The aisles are about 6 feet wide, with half-arched roofs, ribbed in the rock. The *Chaitya* or *Dahgoba* is perfectly plain, with a base, or lower drum, 15¼ feet in diameter; the dome is rather more than half a sphere, and supports the usual capital, consisting of an imitation box, covered by a series of thin square slabs, each projecting a little over the one below it. There is an inscription on the right side of the great arch, which reads:—

वासिठिपुतस कट-
हा दिनो घरमुख
दान

"The gift of a *gṛiha mukha* (cave door or front) by Vasishṭhîputra."

And if we were certain that this were the Vasishṭhîputra Puḷumayi of the Nâsik caves, we might at once refer the inscription to the first half of the second century A.D. The alphabet is quite as old as that. But the terms of the inscription leave the date of the cave doubtful. What does it mean? Did Vasishṭhîputra begin the Chaitya and excavate and carve the façade; or does it not rather imply that he inserted a front? Now on excavating part of the front, I found that a thin wall had been originally left in front, reaching perhaps as high as the spring of the great arch, but this apparently had given way, and a wall, built of immense bricks of admirable colour and texture, had been inserted, several tiers of which still remain *in situ*. This may have been the *gṛiha mukha* given by Vasishṭhîputra. And then the date of the cave itself must be thrown back a considerable period to the age of the Bhâjâ, Kondânê, and Pitalkhorâ chaityas,—or to about the second century B.C.

The Paintings in Cave X.

The whole of the cave has been painted; parts of it more than once. There were, forty years ago, some fine pieces on the side walls, of which few fragments now remain, all having been scribbled over by natives.

The fragments that were visible on the right-hand wall, even twenty years ago, consisted principally of elephants, among which was a large white one with pink spots, and one with six tusks (see Plate VII, fig. 2). They were mostly in outline, but the drawing was strikingly bold and true; on the left was a procession of men, some on foot, some on horseback, variously armed, some with halberts, and differently dressed; and behind were groups of women: but all have been defaced by native visitors within the last twenty years or less. The paintings between the ribs of the roofs in the aisles are principally of Buddhas, and are much more modern. There are also two inscriptions (in one case at least) painted *over* the older work on the walls, but the characters are of much later date than those of Vasishṭhîputra on the façade and one painted inscription to be noticed below.

These paintings are of the earliest period, the dresses of the principal figures belonging to the age of the Sâtakarṇis, and can hardly be attributed to a later date than the latter half of the second century A.D. It is most devoutly to be wished that what still can be recovered may be copied before all is for ever lost.

On the left wall are two drawings of gateways, the patterns of those at Sânchi (see Plate XI, figs. 9 and 10). A little in front of one of them are five or six head-dresses of the age of Sâtakarṇi and many very well drawn faces. Still nearer the front are soldiers with bows and battle axes. The *Bodhidruma* or sacred tree is also painted with offerings hanging from it and people worshipping it (see Plates VIII, IX and X in which a few specimens are given from these very early paintings).

Of later date are the paintings between the ribs of the roof of the aisles, and some inscriptions on a white ground painted over the lower and older portions.

Still nearer the front, however, is a piece of *very* old writing—

Bhagavasa yatipuva deva pavayati patisayasa.

All this combined with the inscription on the left side of the great arch in similar old characters, seems to point to the second century A. D, as the date of these paintings, evidently by far the oldest in the caves, and the dresses agreeing with those in the only other fragment of about the same age in Cave IX.

CAVE XI.

Cave XI. is a Vihâra high up in the rock to the west of No. X. The verandah is supported in front by four plain octagonal columns with bracket capitals and square bases, raised on a panelled base or parapet, similar to what we find in one of the Vihâras at Kârlê and elsewhere. The roof also projects considerably in front of the pillars, and has been very elaborately painted with flowers, birds, and geometrical patterns. The verandah has a cell at either end; that on the right entering in by the side of the hall, whilst the end wall itself is sculptured in three compartments, two with seated Buddhas, attendants, and worshippers, and one with a standing Buddha with *châmara*-bearer and attendant. The door is plainer than in other Vihâras, and the windows are each divided by two pillars into three openings. The hall is 37 feet wide by 28 deep and 10 high, and is supported by four octagonal columns of rather clumsy and primitive style, which leads Mr. Fergusson to thin k this one of the earliest examples of the introduc tion of pillars in Vihâras. There is a sort of seat along the right side of the cave such as we find so frequently in the older caves, and three cells on the left side, also in the back two to the left and one to the right, of the sanctuary, which opens directly from the cave, and is about 12 feet wide by 19¾ deep, with the statue of Buddha separate from the back wall and seated on a *siṅhâsana*, with two well-cut deer on each side of the *chakra* or wheel, and lions behind them. There are no attendant *chaurî*-bearers, but above are flying figures or *gandharvas*. In front of the image is a charmingly natural figure of a man kneeling in adoration, or holding an alms-bowl, the face and hands unfortunately damaged, and probably wilfully. This was, perhaps, intended to represent the excavator of the cave. High up in the wall, and scarcely visible, is an aperture on the left side of the sanctuary, opening into a secret cell.

The Paintings on Cave XI.

The painting in this cave, except in the verandah, is almost entirely gone.

On the roof of the verandah and on the eaves outside the pillars, the painting—much of it of geometrical pattern—is still tolerably entire.

The back wall of the verandah has been much spoilt by some modern *Yogi*, who must have lived here for some time, and has covered the painting with rude *triśulas*, &c. On the left end of it has been a tall standing Buddha on a bluish-black ground, his robe held in his left hand, and flashes of light represented round him.

Above the left window are two sitting figures of Buddha with *châmarawâlâs*; then a painted bracket figure upholding a cross beam (a painted one) ornamented in geometrical patterns. This representation of structural forms in painting does not seem to indicate an early age for the cave.

On a hill, by the side of the door, is an Indra holding some water flowers in his left hand, above are Kinnaras, Apsarâs, Chakravâkas Arhatas, &c.

On the right side of the door has been a similar figure—more destroyed. Over the right window is a fat bracket figure again, and six Buddhas.

This cave has all been painted inside, but it is so much destroyed that no scene can be made out. Much of it seems to have consisted of pictures of Buddha and Bodhisatvas.

CAVES XII and XIII.

Of the five earliest caves, No. VIII to X, XII and XIII, probably the oldest is the *Layana* or Bhikshu's room, No. XIII, though Mr. Fergusson regards No. XII as the oldest vihâra. The latter, however, is a larger cave with some architectural ornament, which inclines me to think it is, if anything, rather the later of the two but not by many years. Both are without pillars inside, and in the cells of both are the stone-couches or beds, which are characteristic of most caves, excavated before the end of the second century, A. D.

The fronts have fallen away from both, but they probably had verandahs with pillars. The hall of No. XIII is only 13½ feet wide by 16½ deep and 7 feet high, and it has seven cells,—three in the left side, and two in the back and right sides.

Cave XII has a hall, about 36½ feet square, with four cells in each of the three inner sides,—eleven of them with double beds, having raised stone-pillows. There are holes in the sills and lintels of the doorways for pivot hinges, and others in the jambs for fastenings. The upper portion of the walls are ornamented over the cell-doors with canopies representing the chaitya-window, with others in the interspaces : the right side wall has two small ones in each interval a graduated pyramidal ornament above (also found on the capital of the *Dahgoba* at the Ganeśa Leṇa, Junnar), and supports or jambs below each small *chaitya*-arch. Below these is a string course wrought with the "Buddhist rail pattern" as in the old vihâra Cave XV at Nâsik, and at Udayagiri,—indeed, as Mr. Fergusson remarks, this cave resembles the latter in almost every respect.

There is a short inscription, in three lines, to the left of one of the cell-doors in the back wall.

CAVE XIV.

Cave XIV is just over XIII, and is reached by a rough ascent over the rock from No. XII. The verandah is 63 feet long by 11 feet, 1 inch wide and 9 feet high, with six pillars and two pilasters in front of it, differing in style from any other here, being square piers, divided by two slightly-sunk fluted bands about 11 inches broad. The body of the capital is vase-shaped, with a flat-inverted shield on each side, and a plain abacus above. Into the cave, which has never been nearly finished, there is a very neat central door and two side ones with two windows. It was intended to be 61 feet wide by 25½ deep, with a row of six columns and two pilasters running along the middle of it, but only the front half has been partially finished. It is probably a very late excavation.

CAVE XV.

The next Vihâra is a few yards farther on. The verandah is about 30 feet long inside by 6½ feet wide, and had two columns and two pilasters; but the front has fallen away—a fragment of one pillar lying in the verandah, showing that they had a torus and fillet at the base, above which they were octagonal, changing to 16 sides, and thence to 32 flutes. The architrave of the door is plain, but the pilasters beyond it are similar to those in other caves. On the upper member of the frieze are carved four birds in low relief. The hall inside has no columns, and is nearly square, 34 feet each way by 10 feet 2 inches high. It has four cells on each side and one at each end of the verandah; the antechamber has two plain pilasters in front and two columns with square bases, then octagonal and sixteen-sided shafts returning through the octagon to square heads. The shrine contains an image of Buddha with the feet turned up on a *siñhâsana*, having only the wheel and lions. It stands against the wall, without attendants, but with small flying *gandharvas* above. In the hall, to the left of the antechamber are two pieces of carving, representing Buddha and attendants. The roof of the antechamber retains only a fragment of painting.

CAVE XVI.

Cave XVI. is another vihâra, and one of the most elegant in its architecture. Its verandah, 65 feet long by 10 feet 8 inches wide, had six plain octagonal pillars with bracket capitals and two pilasters, of which all are gone except one. The cave has a central and two side doors with windows between. The pilasters on each side the principal door are surmounted by female figures standing on the heads of *makaras*. The front aisle is longer than the cave, measuring 74 feet; whilst the body of the hall is 66 feet 3 inches long, by 65 feet 3 inches deep, and 15 feet 3 inches high, supported by twenty octagonal shafts. The middle pair in the front and back rows, however, have square bases, and change first to eight, and then to sixteen sides on the shafts, with square heads and bracket capitals. The roof of the front aisle is cut in imitation of beams and rafters, the ends of the beams being supported by small fat figures as brackets,—in the two central cases single, in the others by two, and in one or two by male and female figures of *Kinnaras*, &c. There are six cells in each side, two in the back wall, and one in each end of the verandah.

The adytum or shrine is entered direct from the hall and has a chamber on each side, separated from it by a screen of two pillars and pilasters. The gigantic statue of Buddha sits with the feet down and the hands in what is called the *dharmachakra mudrâ* or teaching position,—that is, he holds the little finger of the left hand between the thumb and forefinger of the right, with the other fingers turned up. There is a circumambulatory passage or *pradakshiṇâ* quite round the image; and on each side are octagonal pillars screening off side aisles, entered by small doors from the hall, and further lighted by small square windows near the roof.

At the left end of the façade of this cave is an inscription of about twenty-seven lines, unfortunately mutilated, but partially translated by Dr. Bhau Daji. It begins—" Having first saluted (Buddha who is renowned) in this world for the removal of the intense fire of misery of the three worlds.........I shall relate the genealogy of the King Vindhyaśakti, whose power extended over the great," &c. It goes on to mention six or seven other kings of the Vâkâṭakâ dynasty; but most of the names are more or less mutilated; they mostly appear, however, in the Seoni copper-plate grant deciphered by Mr. J. Prinsep, being—

Vindhyaśakti, cir. 400 A.D.
Pravarasena I.
Dêvasena.
Rudrasena I.
Prithivisena.
Rudrasena II.
Pravarasena II.

A fresh transcript of this inscription has been made by Pandit Bhagvanlâl Indraji, and will be translated.

Inside, on the left wall, are two painted inscriptions, both reading—" The charitable assignation of the Sâkya mendicant Bhadanta Dharmadatta. May the merit of this be the cause of attainment of supreme knowledge to mother and to father and to all beings."

The late Rev. Dr. J. Wilson, of Bombay, obtained from Sâgar, a copper-plate grant of this Vâkâṭâka dynasty, which was lent by him to the late Dr. Bhau Daji. Through the kindness of the Hon'ble J. Gibbs, C.S.I., to whom it was handed over by Dr. Bhau Daji's executor, Rao Saheb Vishvanâth Nârâyaṇ Mandlik, I have secured the following transcript of it by Paṇḍit Bhagvanlâl Indraji :—

TRANSCRIPT OF A COPPER-PLATE GRANT OF THE VAKATAKA DYNASTY.

On a seal.

वाकाटकललामस्य
क्रमप्राप्तनृपश्रियः
राज्ञ ✕ प्रवरसेनस्य
शासनं रिपुशासनं

Plate I.

दृष्टं स्वस्ति प्रवरपुरादग्निष्टोमाप्तोर्यामोक्थ्यषोडश्यातिरात्र
वाजपेयबृहस्पतिसवसाद्यस्कचतुरश्वमेधयाजिनः
विष्णुवृद्धसगात्रस्य सम्राट् वाकाटकानां महाराजश्रीप्रवरसेनस्य

सूनोः सूनोः प्रबन्तस्वामिमहाभैरवभक्तस्य सुसंभारसन्निवेशि-
ताशिवलिङ्गोद्वहनशिवसुपरितुष्ट [1]समुत्पादितराजवंशा

Plate II.—First side.

नाम्पराक्रमाधिगतभागीरथ्यमलजलमूर्द्धाभिषिक्तानान्दशा
श्वमेधावभृथस्नातानाम्भारशिवानां महाराजश्रीभवनागदौ
हित्रस्य गौतमीपुत्रस्य पुत्रस्य वाकाटकानां महाराजश्रीरुद्रसे
नस्य सूनोरत्य[2]न्तमाहेश्वरस्य सत्याज्र्जवकारुण्यशौर्यविक्रमन
यविनयमाहात्म्यधीमत्व पात्रागतभक्तित्व धर्मविजयित्व

Plate II.—Second side.

मनोनैर्म्मल्यादि गुणैस्समुपेतस्य वर्षशतमभिवर्द्धमानकोश
दण्डसाधनसन्तानपुत्रपौत्रिणः युधिष्ठिरवृत्ते[3]र्वाकाटका-
नां महाराजश्रीपृथिवीषेणस्य सूनोर्भगवतश्चक्रपाणे ✕ प्रसा
दोपार्जितश्रीसमुदयस्य वाकाटकानां महाराजश्रीरुद्रसेन-
सूनोर्महाराजाधिराजश्रीदेवगुप्तसुतायां प्रभाव-

Plate III.—First side.

तीगुप्तायामुत्पन्न[4]स्य शम्भो ✕ प्रसादधृतिकार्त्तयुगस्य
वाकाटकानाम्परममाहेश्वरमहाराजश्रीप्रवरसेनस्य वचना (त्)
भोजकटराज्ये मधुनदीतटे चर्म्माङ्कनामग्रामः राजमानिकभूमी
सहस्रैरष्टाभिः ८००० शत्रुघ्नराजपुत्रकोण्डराजाविज्ञप्त्या नानागो
त्रचरणेभ्यो ब्राह्मणेभ्यः सहस्राय दत्तः

Plate III.—Second side.

यतोस्मत्सत्तकासर्व्वाध्यक्षा धियोगनियुक्ता आज्ञासञ्चारिकुलपुत्राधिकृता
भटाच्छा[5]त्राश्च विश्रुतपूर्व्वयाज्ञयाज्ञापयितव्या विदितमस्तु वो यथे
हास्माकम्मनोधर्म्मायुर्व्वलविजयैश्वर्य्यविवृद्धये इहामुत्रहिता
र्थमात्मानुग्रहाय वैजेके धर्मस्थाने अपूर्व्वदत्या उदकपूर्व्व
मतिसृष्टः अथास्योचितां पूर्व्वराजानुमतां चातुर्वैद्यग्राममं
र्य्यादा[6]न्वितरामस्तद्यथा अकरदायी अभटछात्रप्रावेश्य

Plate IV.—First side.

अपारंपरगोबलिवर्द अपुष्पक्षीरसन्दोह अचर
सनचर्म्माङ्गार अलवणाक्लिन्नक्रोणिखनकः सर्व्ववेष्टिपरि-

---

[1] Read ष्टि. [2] Read न्त. [3] Read त्तै. [4] Read न्न. [5] Read च्छा. [6] Read दान्वि.

हारपरित्हतः सनिधिस्सोपनिधिःसक्तिप्तापेक्षितः
आचन्द्रादित्यकालीयः पुत्रपौत्र [ा] नुगमकः भुञ्जतां न क-
नचिव्याघात [:] कर्तव्यस्सर्व्वक्रियाभिस्संरक्षितव्य ※ परं वर्द्धयि
[7] तव्वश्च यश्चायं शासनमगणयमानो स्वल्पामपि परिबाधा

Plate IV.—Second side.

[8] न्कुर्यात्कारयिता वा तस्य ब्राह्मणैर्न्निवेदितस्य सदण्डनिग्रहं कुर्य्या
[9] म अस्मिंश्च धर्म्मावरकरणे अतीतानेकराजदत्त सञ्चिन्तन
परिपालनकृतपुण्यानुकीर्त्तनपरिहारर्त्थं न कीर्त्तयामः
व्यासगीतौ चात्र श्लोकौ प्रमाणी कर्त्तव्यौ स्वदत्तांपरदत्तां
[10] व्वा यो हेरत वसुन्धरां गवां शतसहस्रस्य हर्त्तु-

Plate V.—First side.

र्हराति दुष्कृतं षष्टिं वर्षसहस्त्राणि स्वर्गे मोदति भू-
[11] मिदः आच्छेत्ता चानुमन्ता च तान्येव नरके वसेदिति श्शासन-
स्थितिश्चेयं ब्राह्मणैरीश्वरैश्चानुपालनीया तथथा राज्ञां स
[12] म्राङ्गेराज्ये अद्रोहप्रवृन्तानां [अ]ब्रह्मघ्नचौरपारदारिकराजा
पथ्यकारिप्रभृतीनां सङ्ग्राम[म]कुर्व्वतां अन्याग्रामेष्वन

Plate V.— Second side.

[13] पराद्धानां आचन्द्रादित्यकालीयः अतोन्यथा कुर्व्वतामनुमोदतांव्वा
राज्ञः भूमिच्छेदंकुर्व्वतः अस्तेयमिति प्रातिग्राहिणश्चात्र
[14] वारनियुत्ताः शाव्यायनः गणार्य्यः वात्स्यदेवार्यः भारद्वाज
कुमारशर्म्मार्य (:) पाराशर्यगुहशर्म्मा काश्यपदेवार्य्यः माहेश्वरा
[15] मात्रार्य्यः कौण्डिण्यरुद्रार्य्य (:) सोमार्य्य (:) हरिशर्म्मार्य्यर्य्य [16] (:)

Plate VI.—First side.

भारद्वाजकुमारशर्म्मार्य (:) कौण्डिन्य मातृशर्म्मा वरशर्म्मा
गोण्डशर्म्मा नागशर्मा भारद्वा [ज] शान्तिशर्म्मा रुद्रशर्म्मा वात्स्यः
भोजकदेवार्य्य (:) मघशर्म्मा देवशर्म्मा भारद्वाजमोक्षशर्म्मा
रागशर्म्मा रेवतीशर्म्मा धर्म्मार्य (:) भारद्वाजशर्म्मार्य्य (:)
नन्दनार्य्य (:) मूलशर्म्मा ईश्वरशर्म्मा वरशर्म्मा

---

7 Read व्य. 8 Read कुं. 9 Read द. 10 Read वा. 11 Read शा. 12 Read ता. 13 Read वा.
14 Read क्ता. 15 Read न्य. 16 Here र्य्य is erroneously repeated.

Plate VI.—Second side

वात्स्यस्कन्दार्य्य (:) भारद्वाजबप्पार्या (:) धर्म्मार्य्य आत्रेय स्कन्दार्य्य (:)
गौतमसोमशर्म्मार्य्य (:) भर्तृशर्म्मा[17] रुद्रशार्य्य (:) मघार्य्य (:) मातृ
शर्म्मार्य्य (:) ईश्वरशर्म्मार्य्य (:) गौतमसगोत्र मातृशर्म्मार्य्य (:)
कौण्डिन्य देवशर्म्मार्य्य (:) रोहार्य्य (:)

Plate VII.

गौतमसगोत्र स्वामिडार्य्य (:) रेवती शर्म्मार्य्या (:)
ज्येष्ठशर्म्मार्य्य शाण्डिल्यकुमारशर्म्मार्य्य (:) स्वातीशर्म्मा-
र्य्य (:) शाट्यायणकौण्डार्य्य प्रभृतय: सेनापती
चित्रवर्म्मणि संवत्सरेष्टादशे १८ ज्येष्ठमासशुक्ल
पक्षत्रोदश्यां शासनं लिखितमिति

Until we know more about this Vâkâṭakâ dynasty it is impossible to fix a date with confidence to the last on the above list, but from the style of architecture and of the alphabet used in the inscription we may, with very considerable probability assign this cave to a date very near to 500 A.D.

A stair leads down from the front of this cave, and turns to the left into a chamber on the back wall of which, on excavation, was found a Nâga Râja, (Plate XIII., fig. 1) seated, like Vishṇu in the left end of the verandah of the great cave at Bâdâmi upon the coils of the snake whose hoods canopy his high, flat-topped *mukuṭa*. A door leads out from the front of this room flanked outside by two elephants in *basso rilievo*, and from this the stair descended to the river.

The Paintings in Cave XVI.

The whole has been covered with painting, though it is now much destroyed. The roof of the verandah was painted in square and circular compartments; and in the hall the sides of the columns were painted with flowers and scrolls.

There is still, however, a good deal of painting left inside which the ravages of bats and nest-building insects are helping to destroy, and which would have been partially prevented if Mr. Griffiths's judicious advice to provide wooden doors and windows had been carried out. It is only Caves I, II, XVI and XVII that greatly need this protection, and it is to be hoped the Government of His Highness the Nizam will see the propriety of it, and of providing more effectively for the protection of the caves against the carelessness as well as the vandalism of natives, such as Nârâyan Ekanâth, the Peśkar of Ajaṇṭâ, who of late years has done so much injury to the frescoes in this and in Cave XVII.

I.

A fragment of the ceiling decoration in the verandah remains pretty entire and is of such merit as to deserve copying.

II.

On the architrave, over the bracket of one of the front pillars of the verandah, is a figure of a *Bhikshu* sleeping and a wild beast licking his feet, while

[17] Read र्तृ.

a horse stands behind him. To the right is another *Bhikshu* seated and two men before him, while the wild beast comes in from the right. Over another bracket are two *Bhikshus*, a woman, and some other figures.

III.

On the left end of the back wall of the verandah is a piece of painting. Above, Buddha sits on a throne, in bluish robe (much defaced) ; on his left side are fragments of three figures wearing crowns (one has a green skin) ; and on the other is some great person and a number of females bearing gifts.

Below is another Buddha standing and facing the right, in front of a green niche, over which is the umbrella. To the left are four figures wearing crowns, and behind them eighteen others, one fairer and larger than the rest, but all richly jewelled,—evidently great people or *râja-kumâras*. To the right of Buddha are some six *jaṭâ*—wearing light, orange-skinned attendants,—one with a nimbus, and one with a *châmara*. Still to the right, are five smaller figures, and above a green man, while in the back ground is a defaced figure (as of Garuḍa) with a snake in his hand. The figures in this lower portion seem all to be presented against a back ground of clouds.

Above the side door is also a figure like Buddha in the clouds.

IV.

In the left end of the front aisle is a very curious piece of painting, the interest of which seems to centre in a child, held by the hands and feet by a man and woman, while a third seems about to cut it in two with a sword.

Above, two ranges of hills are represented in the usual fashion, and between them a river. Below, near the right hand side, is a country cart drawn by men ; above, on the hill, is a man wearing a Persian cap who seems to be in grief ; a green man stands near—carrying another (perhaps the same) up the hill. Still higher, the man in the Persian cap sits with two others paying respect to a small red figure on a rock, who holds the little finger of his left hand with the right and addresses them. Beside, or to the left of the three, stands a green man with long streaming hair, and behind him is a figure with a sword. In the back-ground are plantain trees indicative of a wood-land scene.

More of this tableau would be brought out if varnished, and it deserves early copying. There are some figures on the return of the front wall also which may merit attention.

V.—The Dying Princess.

To the right of the pilaster is the painting of 'the dying princess' [1] :—A lady of rank sits on a couch leaning her left arm on the pillow and an attendant behind holds her up. A girl in the back-ground places her hand on her breast and looks towards the lady. Another, with a sash across her breast, wields the *pankhâ*, and an old man in white cap looks in at the door, while another sits beside a pillar. In the foreground sit two women. In another apartment are two figures ; one with a Persian cap has a water vessel (*kalaśa*) and a cup in the mouth of it ; the other, with negro-like hair, wants something from him. To the right two *kanchukinîs* sit in a separate apartment. Mr. Griffiths very justly remarks on this picture that "for pathos and sentiment and the unmistakeable way of telling its story this picture, I consider, cannot be surpassed in the history of art. The

[1] This picture was copied by Mr. Griffiths in 1872-73.

Florentine could have put better drawing, and the Venetian better colour, but neither could have thrown greater expression into it."

"The dying woman with drooping head, half-closed eyes, and languid limbs, reclines on a bed, the like of which may be found in any native house of the present day. She is tenderly supported by a female attendant, whilst another, with eager gaze, is looking into her face, and holding the sick woman's arm as if in the act of feeling her pulse. The expression on her face is one of deep anxiety as she seems to realize how soon life will be extinct in the one she loves. Another female behind is in attendance with a *pankhâ*, whilst two men on the left are looking on with the expression of profound grief depicted in their faces. Below are seated on the floor other relations, who appear to have given up all hope, and to have begun their days of mourning, for one woman has buried her face in her hand and apparently is weeping bitterly."

VI.

Above No. 5 is a large palace or a *vihâra*. In it, near the middle, is Buddha, in his white robe with his begging-bowl in his hand, and again he appears in the door-way to the left. To the right of the first a number of Bhikshus look out of the doors. Again, to the right and below, Buddha stands holding out his begging dish, and at his feet a râja kneels and makes obeisance (see Plate XIV, fig. 3).

Behind, to the left, are other sitting figures. Above on the right, a figure with Persian cap, on horseback, enters a gate; one with a similar cap, and one without, are beyond it. Farther on, to the left, re-appear the same figure, and the horse neighing, and a man with them having a striped *dhôtî*, while three figures in caps appear outside and a fourth holds another horse. Below is a man with a crooked sword and another with a Persian cap following him.

A piece of the plaster has disappeared below this, and lower still a râja is shown and two or three figures—one with a long straight sword.

Between the first and second cell-doors has been a *vihâra* with Buddha in the centre of it, and females in the side divisions. One of them in the transparent garb of nobility. This piece has been much defaced of late. Mrs. Spier's wood-cut from Major Gill's copy is given (Plate XIII, fig. 2).

Near the roof, to the right, is a *Gandharva* and *Apsarâ*, and to the right is a hill on which are two monks talking and a third sitting by. Below this the plaster has fallen off, but to the right is a vihâra. On the left side of it sits Buddha or some monk, and in the foreground another with a look of wonder. In front a man is seated, apparently in deep grief, while another stands behind him. In the *vihâra* on the left, stands a *Bhikshu*, and behind him a bald-headed monk sits in distress. In the right side sit other two, and two stand behind them. In a niche (*gokhlê*) in the wall above, two jugs are represented.

VII.

To the right, over the third cell-door, are four Buddhas, each with three umbrellas and underneath three painted Sanskrit inscriptions.

Above are seven more Buddhas and a short painted inscription.

VIII.

Beyond the fourth cell-door Buddha sits on a *siñhâsana*, the lions on which are almost pictures of the Assyrian bull figures. His feet are on a lotos, the stalk of it supported by Nâga Râjas. His attendants also stand on lotoses. The lion is shown, Plate XIV, fig. 4.

IX.

On the left end of the back wall is a similar figure with Lôkêśvara on his left, and a Bhikshu with a *mâlâ* on his right hand, as attendants. To the right, near the cell-door, are a number of sitting figures.

X.

Between the cell-door and the antechamber is a large scene with five elephants above, and others below, ridden by râjas with great retinues, the attendants with musical instruments, and soldiers with long blue curved swords. One figure below on a horse has the regal umbrella carried over his head.

XI.

On the other side of the antechamber has been a similar scene with figures having bows, spears, swords and shields, two of the latter with huge "bogie" faces on their fronts. To the right a number of women follow bearing a *pankhâ*, vessels, &c.

XII.

Between the doors of the first and second cells on this side has been a grand scene, in which Buddha is enthroned and teaches a great assembly, all wearing *mukuṭas*; perhaps they are the Devas in the Tushita, heaven. The picture is much defaced however.

XIII,

The right wall contained some very interesting paintings which—to the disgrace of the Ajaṇṭâ Peśkar—have been much ruined, within the last seven years by his cutting out portions of them, especially faces to present to visitors in order to secure a present!!

Much, however, is still left, especially on the upper portions of the wall, but the colours are so flat that, until they are varnished, it is impossible to make out the different scenes.

Between the third and fourth doors in this side aisle is the famous scene of the visit of Asita to the infant Buddha,[1] a story so paralled to that of Simeon, that one can scarcely suppose it a coincidence but a borrowed episode.

In a palace a Brahman is seated, and in front a boy (Buddha) sits on a stool with a board in his hands, above his head is a cage of birds, and a *ravâja* or musical instrument, and round him sit three others with boards.

To the left, Asita is seated holding the infant Buddha in his hands (Plate XIV, fig. 5) and before him Buddha's father and mother, while in the foreground is Asita's disciple or *Śishya*.

XIV.

Below No. 13 is Buddha shooting (Plate XIV, fig. 6) and other boys sitting behind him, while his teacher sits a little to the right. To the left are also some boys sitting together.[1]

Above, to the right, is the scene in the bedroom, when Buddha left his wife and infant son to become a monk. The rest requires restoration before any account can be given of it.

---

[1] Of this picture Dr. Bhau Daji had a fine copy, from which it would be of importance to obtain a duplicate.

CAVE XVII.

The next Cave is another fine Vihâra cave similar to the last and apparently executed about the same time. Mr. Fergusson considers these two caves as the most interesting in the series.

Outside to the left, over a cistern, and under the inscription is a triple compartment of sculpture: in the centre Buddha squats under an ornamental arch or *toraṇa*, with *Vidyâdharas* above, and wheel, deer, and lions below. On each side is a Buddha standing on a lotos with worshippers below. At the right end, opposite this, several rows of squatting Buddhas have been sculptured on the rock, a piece of which has broken and fallen away, leaving a higher portion to slide down. A stair leads down from the front of the cave and must have descended to the stream.

The verandah has been supported by six plain octagonal columns with bracket capitals and neat bases resembling the Attic base, but without its lower torus. The hall is entered by a central door, resembling that in No. XVI, with a row of painted Buddhas over it, and by two side doors. It is further lighted by two windows. This apartment is 63¾ feet wide by 62 feet deep, and 13 feet high, its roof being supported by twenty octagonal pillars,—all plain, except the two in the middle of the front and back rows, which have square bases, shafts partly octagonal and partly 16 sided and more ornamented. The antechamber is small with two pillars in front,—but the shrine is 17¾ feet wide by 20 deep, and in front of the great image there stands on the floor two figures, one holding the alms-bowl of the *Bhikshu*, the other damaged. There are also two attendants on each side of the Buddha and two *chaurî*-bearers.

Besides the two in the verandah, this cave contains sixteen cells. At the right end of the verandah there is a small hole in the floor into a fine cistern of water, the entrance to which is up a flight of steps between this cave and No. XVI.

There is an inscription at the left end of the verandah, outside, of about the same length as that on Cave XVI. Dr. Bhau Dâji's translation of it gives us the names of certain princes—

Dhritarâshtra,
his son *Hari Samba*,
his son *Kshitipâla Sauri Samba*,
Upendragupta, and
his son *Skacha*.

Of these we know nothing more: they may have been petty râjas of the sixth century. Bhagvanlâl Indraji has taken a new impression of this inscription.

The Paintings in Cave XVII.

In this there is more painting than in any other of the caves, and much of it is still in a condition to be copied, but the bats are making sad ravages in it, and it is a thousand pities, this has not been put a stop to long ago; the Peśkar has also made sad havoc of some of the paintings. In no country but India, where so very few have any regard for art or antiquities, would such a work have been so long left totally uncared for.

I.

The so-called Zodiac in the left end of the verandah seems to be some sort of representation of the world. Had there been nine divisions, it might have been interpreted as the nine *khandas* of Jambudvipa, but there were only eight, and the various ways in which the persons in each are engaged seem to indicate different aspects of worldly life. The few figures [1] now left are small, but sufficiently clearly painted, to be made out. The outer edge or rim of the wheel is divided into sixteen compartments, each containing a symbol, such as a monkey, a man, &c. This wheel is held up by two long green arms with bracelets.

II.

To the left, on the same wall, are two bullocks led by a man, a woman carrying some object on a board on her head, and two red-skinned men, one with a bhangy over his shoulder: these are a continuation of No. 3 beneath. Below is a *Bhikshu* seated in a cave with a water-pot in front and a dead body at his feet. Below this is a green-skinned râja and attendants much defaced, but with the name *Mânibhadra*, written under his seat. On the right is a *Bhikshu*, with a jug on a stand, talking to a laic seated before him.

III.

To the left, on the return of the wall above, is a large orange-coloured snake, encircling an area with men, buildings, and trees in it. The scene extends on to the edge of the large circle on the end wall, as already stated (see Plate. XVI).

IV.

Below the last is painted the Litany of Avalôkitêśvara, unfortunately all but totally obliterated. Avalôkitêśvara holds the palm of his right hand forward, and has a bottle with oval body and narrow neck in his left. Of the oval compartments at each side only a few can be partially made out: the upper one on the left represents a raging fire and a figure fleeing from it to Avôlakitêśvara and the next seems to have been Dharani, Kâlî, or Death, pursuing her victim. On the right, the upper picture contained the snake as the enemy from which deliverance was to be sought; the next a lion; and the third an infuriated elephant.

V.

On the back wall of the verandah at the extreme left end, is a young râja seated; and his râni on his right, and another female with only a white and blue petticoat and rich pearl necklace. Below is a woman with a dish (*kunda*) and before the râja a red-skinned man laying off some story; behind is another red man in white *aṅgarkha*, listening interestedly, as if he were the partner of the speaker. In front of him is a green man with a stick, facing round to a *Bhikshu* who, with six others, (two with square umbrellas and one with fair hair) seem to wait for something. One older than the rest has a stick. Above these last are five men on seats, one red, probably a householder, and the rest *Bhikshus*—one white-skinned and his hair in the *jaṭâ* style. Before them are dishes, and three small and one large cup by each, with flowers; and on the left is one vessel set above another with flowers in it. Two females present flowers in vases. On the left a man comes in bearing a bhangy with *gharâs* or water-vessels. To the right of the woman is a greenish man, dressed in

[1] When Mr. Ralph visited the caves in 1828 he counted 73 figures in three of the compartments, varing from 5 to 7 inches in height, and apparently only about a third of it was then wanting; a mere fragment now remains.

striped garment, holding a white dish, and in front of him another—also with a dish—serving the *Bhikshus*. To the left are two beggars (one has but one eye) then a third red one-eyed fellow, and next two women—one in a sort of sack (*kantha*), peaked head-dress, and very fair ; the other with a jacket, &c., and a child on her hip. Above her is another bearing something like a shield with a fringe, and on her right a fair figure. All these seem to be begging. In the foreground is a man on a pinkish horse and another about to mount one. To the right of this latter horse is a man with a bason and two in front of him begging.

VI.

Over the right jamb of the side door and extending over the window is another scene. In a palace (over the window) a brown-skinned râja treats his fair wife, in gauzy *sâḍî*, to some sherbet. A Persian servant, in green, with an elegant claret jug, enters to supply more. A little red dwarf holds a spittoon and another spittoon is at the râja's side. Behind a *kanchukinî* or servant brings in some dish or other object. On the left, two women look out at a window, and on the right two others and a man stand in the verandah. On each side the palace are *Bêla* trees.

Leaving the palace on the left, is a lady of distinction with a woman carrying an umbrella over her head, and behind them a servant: beside the lady and holding her by the hand, is a reddish *Kanchukinî*, distinguished by her full dress in blue and white ; then a fair man bearing a bow and some bulky objects. Behind him are two women, the red one with a dish of flowers ; and then the brown râja with an umbrella carried over his head. In the foreground two women (their heads now gone) stand near the gateway, outside which is the Darwân observing them coming. Beside the gate is a plantain or *kêlâ* plant.[1]

VII.

To the right of the window is some mountain scene. In front was a gigantic green-skinned râja with magnificent head-dress, now nearly gone. Up at the roof is the *Jonesia Aśoka* tree, and in front of it a pea-fowl with white wings, blue beak and breast, and green tail. Before it is perhaps a water-runnel, which a monkey approaches from behind another *Aśoka* tree with the buds scarcely burst. Above are two *Kinnaras* with human busts and birds' feet and tails ; one with cymbals, and the other with some other instrument. To the left, on blue clouds, is a fair *Gandharva* with a basket over the shoulder and three *apsarâs* —one with cymbals and the other with *bañsi*, and two attendants—one with a sort of *vina*, another with a sword (*talwâr*) and a crown. Below is a red pair of *Kirâtas*—the man with a bow. The rest is destroyed.

On the extreme right two comical little figures (*Guhyakas*) sit on a rock.

VIII.

By the edge of the door are some fragments of painting. On the frieze of the door are eight Buddhas—the seventh S'âkya Simha under a pipal tree and the eighth Maitrêya or Dipankara Buddha with a high *mukuṭa*, and each under his *bodhi* tree.

---

[1] The *Ratnâvali* mentions it as *kadali*.

IX.

On the lintel are eight compartments, each containing a pair of figures, treating each other to liquor,—the women mostly redder than the men. The jambs have been painted in neat patterns.

X.

On the right of the door above, are some *gandharvas*, and below them a *bhikshu*. To the right is a mountain scene with a large royal, orange-coloured, figure in front, and above to the right a *Yaksha* and two *Apsarâs* with remarkable head-dresses (Plate XVII, fig 1). Below (perhaps in a cave) are two *Kinnaras*. Under the *Yaksha* are two blue pea-fowls, and under them is a Bhill (bowman) crouching forward; and lower still the heads of two figures.

XI.

Over the two windows to the right is painted a story. First, over the left window is King Bimbisara seated in his palace, with a pillow behind him and his wives and one *Kanchukinî* on his right; on his left is a *bhikshu* or his diwân. In a floor below are three women and a man, and to the right is the door and porter or *darwân*. In the compound are some men sitting, and three horses and an elephant looking out of the stables. Then a doorway and the Bazar, in which are seen women looking out of windows with sunshades over them. Two horses go towards the palace and between them a light-coloured elephant proceeding from the palace seizes a *bhikshu* in his trunk. Then, (over the second window) the same elephant kneels at the feet of Buddha and his disciple (*śishya*), perhaps Ananda or Sariputra, both with alms-bowls (see Plate XVII, fig. 2). Many men in the bazar are looking on with interest, and two behind Buddha are fleeing from the elephant.

XII.

On the end wall is Vaibhâra hill. Buddha is throned in front and many râjas, among which are two distinguished over the rest by their jewellery. On clouds are *arhats* with *jaṭâ* head-dresses. The story is well known in the life of Buddha in connection with Râjagṛiha. Two chataks (or *chakravâkas*) are on each side of Buddha.

XIII.

In the right jamb of the last window is Manjughosha—Min-nâtha as he is called in Nepal with a jug in his left hand—the oval, resembling a glory round him—is the representation of the stone cut away in forming a carved image. He is the disciple of Matsyendranâtha, and at the present day his car is drawn after Matsyendarnâtha's in processions in Nepal.

XIV.

In the first of the two windows is a Buddha on the left jamb with his alms-bowl. On the other is also a Buddha (defaced) and an attendant.

XV.

The ceiling of the verandah, copied by Major Gill, is now in the India Museum at Kensington. In the centre, six figures have six arms between them, and had perhaps only two feet, but the middle portion of it is gone long ago.

XVI.

The roofs of the aisles are tolerably entire, but the colouring has been so damaged by smoke that only the designs can now be made out.

The roof of the central area is in a similar condition. If differs from the other roofs in a very large portion of the area having been filled by concentric circles, decorated in various patterns, and then a broad square border outside, filled with animal and other figures, among which a cock-fight and a ram contest are prominent.

XVII.

The pillars also have been painted, and large portions of the decorations on them can still be made out, and are very interesting. The figures of lions, and grotesque beings on the bases of some of them are quite unique. It is a pity we have not restorations of one or two of them.

XVIII.

In the left end of the front aisle and left side of the cell door is a scene in a palace. Towards the right side of the picture a crowned râja sits, holding a sheathed sword with his left hand, and apparently about to draw it with the right. Behind him stand two females, the first with a *chaurî*, the second, darker in complexion, and with a royal head-dress. Before the râja, on the left, and very close to him, stands a man dressed as a Brâhman Bhikshu, with a white sheet over his left shoulder and under his right arm, bare head, a small ring in his ear and small moustache. He appears to lean with his left elbow on the râja's seat, and holds the other up to his chin. His nails are remarkably long. Just behind him is a black servant who might pass for a Habshi or even a negro, with curly hair carrying some hidden object on his back, by the loop of the fastening which comes over his left shoulder. In his ears are long earrings, and in his left hand a sort of foil or wand. He is naked to the waist and wears striped short drawers.

Still to the left is another râja standing. Behind him an attendant with small moustache appears to be carrying some object, and behind, in the door, is a porter. To the right of the râja is seen a *châmara*, and the head of a lady with royal head-dress.

Above, on the eaves of the roof, is a bird *(chakravaka)*, and on a frieze, a little higher, an elephant fight is represented as carved—like those in caves I and VI.

Over this, from a window, six ladies look out, one apparently in grief, who points downwards.

Over this again is an inscription in red paint but not original.

Below all this are to be traced the crowns and part of the heads of two persons, one of whom has a nimbus *(bhamaṇḍala)* and like Śiva, a third eye in his forehead, but horizontal.

XIX.

On the right side of the cell, about the level of the top of the door, a râja sits, a dark female behind him has the *châmara*, and behind her to the left another holds the umbrella. To the right sit four men, pale and red-skinned, and one green with moustaches and with a blue water lily (a red man also has a water lily), and another red one behind is more richly dressed. The one to the right is clothed to the neck, wears stockings and seems to speak to the râja. Behind him is a fair female servant bringing in a tray of flowers, and beyond her is a green one. To the right is another green one with a *châmara*.[1] To the right and a little lower are two geese (*haṅsa*) on seats and on the return of the pilaster, are some seven *haṅsas*, while lower still a man bears two in his hands.

Under the râja, to the left, is mountain scenery with plants in flower and a lake with water flowers (*kamala*) and geese in it.

Above is more painting, tolerably entire, but so dirty from bats' and birds' dung, that until thoroughly cleaned and varnished, nothing can be seen of it.

XX.

On the front of the pilaster Buddha is represented seated, in a red robe, with nimbus round his head and two Lôkêśvaras as *châmara*-bearers by him.

XXI.

On the left of the first cell-door, in the left aisle, a lady sits on a large seat with a *mukuṭa* on her head, and on her left, behind the seat, stands an attendant. On the return of the pilaster, to the left, is another woman seated, not so richly dressed, and behind her, a third stands looking towards the left.

Below the first part of this is a lake with *kamala* flowers, and beside it are men and a woman.

XXII.

To the right of the first cell-door—the scene extending[2] to the next—is a Rânî who seems to have entered from a door on the left. To the right is the Râja standing with an attendant behind him, below to the right are two children perhaps royal, for the Râja takes one of them by the hand. Above are two men, one perhaps a suppliant, and to the left a round object, but whether a shield or some sort of round fan is not very clear. To the right stand two men talking—one of them like a Brâhman. Behind them are two horses, and still to the right, are three men, one with a spotted bag at his side, and below are some fragments of other figures.

XXIII.

Between the second and third cell-doors are two horses and a man leading them. In the foreground to the right are two persons of distinction who meet an oldish man, with a rosary, coming from a rocky hill. To the right of him are the heads of two more horses. Lower and to the right a figure sits under a roof, or perhaps in a cave, with a tree or bush to the right of it; and below are some figures not easily made out.

XXIV.

Between the third and fourth cell-doors are a series of acts in which an old man, bald on the forehead, with prominent teeth and square umbrella in his hand, apparently begging, appears at least four times. First, to the right of the upper half of the third cell door, he seems to enter from the left and to address a wealthy man, by whom sits his wife, looking round at the man. Behind is an-

---

[1] If carefully cleaned and varnished, this would come out well.

[2] This fine scene should be copied as soon as possible.

other man and further to the right, the porter. Lower and to the right the beggar appears again with bag and jug on his back, before a figure dressed as a râja with an attendant seated at his foot, while a girl looks at the old man from the left.

Lower again and to the left a man is represented, giving him a water *kalaśa*.

At the upper right hand, in a palace, a râja richly jewelled, sits with a *châmara-wâlî* behind him and another attendant bringing forward a vessel, while the man appears again on the left begging; on the extreme right sits a lady, while a child rests against the râja's cushion.

Below, a richly-jewelled man sits to the left of a green one, and to the right is a third.

All this might probably be made out with a little care.

There is also much painting on the upper part of this wall, but it is so smoked that perhaps it could not now be copied.

XXV.

In the end of the back aisle, above the cell-door, are many horses, with riders at the gallop and some archers among them, but the painting is so blackened as not to be easily made out.

Below on the left side of the cell-door, a wild man, his hair on end, heaves a large stone at a great monkey lying asleep. To the left, another man (or perhaps the same) appears as if about to seize a monkey who sits looking round, with a large stone beside him. To the left is a tree and a deer and other animals beyond it.

Beneath, the sleeping monkey is another, stretching up his hands and a man near him. And from the left another large one advances with a man behind him.

XXVI.

On the back wall, from the corner to the door of the first cell, is a pretty large piece of wall painting. In the upper right corner a man of some note sits under a canopy with his wife to the right, while another greenish female to the left, with her hair in a fillet, seems to speak earnestly to him. Another seems to be approaching in front and holding up her hands in astonishment or terror. Behind her is a green woman and a man with a woman before him who holds two objects like the heads of two crocodiles or *makaras*, perhaps musical instruments.

To the left a red man, bald, and with a circle on the side of his head, looks back excitedly, and in front of him a woman presents her joined palms to the left, while she looks to the right. Still to the left are two men, one with a mace in his hand. Near the left wall are the faces of other two figures; but a piece of the plaster has been wickedly cut out here, probably like others, by the Péskar.

XXVII.

Below the last, to the left is a palace in which sits a râja with two female attendants and in front of him two men, to whom he seems to be talking. Below he is again represented sitting under a roof with several female attendants. From the gate on the left, a horse goes out (the rider now destroyed), and beyond it is another horseman. Above, an elephant leaves the palace, the rider holding an *ankuśa* or goad in his hand, while four soldiers (*sipahis*) march forward with shields and swords, the two in front apparently turning away from the spectator, and a râja upon an elephant is meeting them. Above this the painting, though pretty entire, is too much blackened by smoke to be made much of.

XXVIII.

Between the first and second cell-doors on the back wall is a large and animated tableau. On the upper left side, a râja sits on his throne in a palace, behind him is a green *châmara*-bearer and another reddish female, to the left (of his head) was another—(whose head has been shamefully cut out like others); and beside her a fair *kanchukinî*. In front of the râja, on a stool, sits a red-skinned man, without jewellery, and with a cloth over his left shoulder, and behind him, to the left, stand ten similarly dressed like Brahmanical Bhikshus. In front of them are two men, one carrying some object, and dressed in full white garments, as porters usually are; the other perhaps a sipâhi of the body-guard. The man before the râja, seems to look back and speak to them. Above the heads of the Bhikshus a number of horses look out at stable windows (see Plate XVIII.)

Below, in another apartment, a red man on the left seizes another by the waist-band, who in turn seizes the next to the left and strikes him so that he is falling prone. A fourth turns round on the second, and to the left three more struggle together (see Plate XVIII.)

Below this is a great *sowâri*. The râja has come out of the gate on the right, on horseback, with the umbrella over him, and his diwân riding behind. A dozen men with spears in their hands advance in front; two more have swords and shields, and with dogs. To the left is a jungle and mountains, and in the mountains are deer, who run before the huntsmen, and two tigers couch in their lairs. The râja seems to have gone off in front after the deer. Above, to the left, a man sleeps in the jungle with his weapon besides him, while a tiger or lion licks his feet. A little above a man sits with his sword at his side and his horse at his left, while a lion appears in front of him. Probably he is the râja of the hunting scene. Still higher, a great *sowâri* of horses, elephants, spearmen, &c., proceed to the right towards a scene where flags are displayed and women sit on the top of the palace to see the hunt, while beyond them in the background, a huge lion passes.

To the right, above the cell-door, are some more figures.

XXIX.

To the right of the second cell-door, and between it and the antechamber, under a *mandap*, upon a seat, is a râja, on whose head two men pour vessels of water, performing his *abhisheka*. On the right a female, with a tray in her left hand, offers him a flower, and three other figures appear below to the left.

In a house to the right are seven figures, apparently of different ages; the biggest has got some object in his hands and the smallest two arrows, or something like them. Below this, on the left appear two men on elephants, and another of very marked features riding with a *chhatra* carried behind him, with another horseman following. Below are about a dozen soldiers, with spears, shields, swords, &c.,—all apparently directing an attack on a tall crowned râja, who seems to come out of a palace, and who is in act to throw a javelin at them and seems to have killed two. Probably this is the same râja as is receiving his *abhishekha* above.

On the right side of this scene, another piece of plaster has been cut out by the same vandal as destroyed the others.[1]

XXX.

On the left end of the antechamber is a very interesting scene, which it seems most desirable to have copied soon, before it suffer more.

Below, Buddha sits in the middle in the *dharmachakra mudrâ*; two celestial *chaurî-bearers* stand by his side; and above, the usual *vidyâdhara* on clouds are bringing garlands. On the right side, about sixteen *Bhikshus* sit, all bareheaded and dressed alike. Above them are three horses, on one of which is a man in Iranian dress with peaked cap, jerkin, and trowsers; and in the back-ground behind these, is an elephant on which sits a great lady with her children and the *dâsîs* behind her, all making obeisance (*namaskâra*) to Buddha.

At Buddha's feet two râjas sit making profound obeisance.

On the left side, among a crowd of notables, a great râja, of youthful appearance, sits on a cushion, making his obeisance. To the right and behind him are two with smaller crowns, the one to the right also on a cushion. To the left is another with a small crown and beyond him a decidedly Persian personage, with high peaked cap, short black beard, and long hair; while in front of him a jewelled *râjakumâra* is seated. To the left are four horsemen one bearded and completely clothed, probably a servant of the prince or chief.

Behind the whole group are two more Sassanians and two horses, the riders on which have the Sassanian dress and peaked caps.

Above are two elephants, on one of which is a man, bareheaded, and with the Sassanian ribbons or 'banderoles' at the back of his neck, while a curious-looking attendant behind him makes *namaskâra*, like the rest. On the other elephant are several Sassanian people, all engaged in the same way, while three pennants are carried over their heads and three spears in front, with tassels attached to them. In the background beyond this elephant, another fair Sassanian carries an umbrella.

XXXI.

In the scene above the last, Buddha stands surrounded by four *Arhats* and two *Bodhisattvas*.

XXXII.

On the left of the shrine door, stands a colossal Buddha with his alms-bowl in his hand, while to the left in a doorway is a lady with a Japanese-like countenance, pushing foward a child to put some alms in Buddha's bowl. In a window above is a *kalaśa*. This is a most interesting little scene full of true feeling: it is repeated, in sculpture, to the right of the door in Cave XIX.

XXXIII.

The right end of the antechember is painted with standing and sitting Buddhas,—the lower portion, however, is destroyed, except a fragment at each end. That portion remaining at the right side is very curious,[2] representing a number of Digambara Jaina *bhikshus* helping forward an old fat one, and carrying the *rajoharna* or *pichhi*—a besom to sweep away insects, &c. Most of them are

---

[1] On the wall plans, Plates XII and XV, the pieces cut out are marked *a*, *a*.

[2] This should be copied.

shaven-headed and stark naked. One or two who wear their hair are clothed. On the extreme left is an elephant and a horse with two men. The intermediate painting is completely destroyed.

XXXIV.

The upper portion of the walls of the back and sides of the cave are so smoked, that it is almost impossible to make anything out of them. The plaster, however, is tolerably entire, and possibly careful cleaning may recover some scenes.

On the bases of the two pillars and pilasters of the antechamber are figures in which a deal of weird drollery is displayed. That on the right pilaster is a large face with heavy wig and a mouse or rat in the ear for a jewel, the necklace bears a crab as a pendant, and a hideous face on the belly has a snake in its ear.

The pillars of the antechamber have two similar ogre figures each on their bases.

XXXV.

To the right of the antechamber, the painting is mostly peeled off, but the lower margin of it shows several small animals—and above is the top of a palace with three domes, each with a high pinnacle, and slender spires at the corners, the balustrade having *chaitya*-window ornaments.

Above this, to the right, a dark man is presenting some white object to a red-skinned one who is seated. Further to the right are two men on horseback and others on foot, a large dog, and other figures. Then, nearly over the second cell-door, is a pool, and a man, apparently riding on a deer, which also appears again below with a burden. Still to the right is another tank with birds and fishes in it. All these are much smoked.

XXXVI.

Between the cell doors, is a large picture with one piece wilfully cut out of it.

On the left, below, is a râja coming out of a gate on horseback, with a servant behind carrying the *chhatrî*, and four others—two with swords and one with a spear,—also another horseman beyond. They seem to pursue a large light-coloured elephant without any housings. In front, three spearmen run at full speed for the jungle to the right, where two elephants seem to have seized the first by the leg. To the left again, below, the elephant rushes off, pursued by the râja, while in front are two men on horseback.

XXXVII.

Above on the left of the last scene, a râja is seated on his throne, and behind him stand three women, one with a *chaurî*. On the right are other two women ; and a man sits in front on a stool.

To the right again, the râja stands with a number of attendants round him, and in the door to the right is the porter. Outside is the elephant, and behind it two tame ones, housed and mounted with the three spearmen beside them ; and in the door to the right is a sort of trough on wheels, and a large vessel which two men seem to be taking out to feed the elephant from. Outside is a man carrying perhaps two bundles of grass or leaves on a *bhangi*.

XXXVIII.

On the right side of the second cell door, where another piece has also been destroyed by the same boor as the others, is left the head of a horse on which a man was approaching a *Yogi* in the jungle. Below, the horse is again seen, and the man kneeling before the Yogi, to whom another, in white clothes, brings a dead body with *jaṭa* head-dress and red loin cloth. Below again, by a hill, a man in the same Yogi dress is carrying a man and woman in the scales of a *bhangi*.

XXXIX.

In the back aisle, on the left side of the cell door, in a jungle, is a monkey and an ox. Below the monkey is again painted as having got on its back and put its hands on the eyes of the ox.

XL.

On the front of the back pilaster has been a female standing figure in a panel, and below and above are bands of various tints. Under the bracket is another piece of painting now stained and discoloured.

XLI.

On the side of the pilaster facing the front of the cave, above, is a red female demon (*Râkshasî*) flying in the clouds and holding a man over her shoulder by the ancle. Below is another, of white colour, with long tusks, large eyes, and dishevelled hair; behind her is a third darker demon also flying, and a fourth to the left.

XLII.

Below the last is a tall single standing man of a dusky complexion, richly jewelled with a rich waist-chain holding up a short *dhôtî* or striped drawers, and with a flower in his right hand.[1]

XLIII.

Over the fourth cell door in the aisle, is a large building or palace. In the left of the three compartments into which it is divided are three women, two standing, one of them in rich dress, and one sitting.

In the central apartment is a reddish Rákshasí standing with a dagger in her hand. In front a white one sits with a child in her lap, and on each side sits a green female companion. These four seem to be the same figures as on the side of the pilaster in No. 41.

In the third apartment the white demon has a cup and is drinking from it, while two dark females stand behind.

Below this, a red female demon, her hair streaming backwards, and with in her right hand something which seems to be falling off, perhaps flesh, and a white companion, are shown flying upwards. To the left, over the cell-door, are two horrid white female demons, each with a cup—a red and a striped one—held in their long claws, and their hair streaming upwards,—the front one looking back. They seem to proceed over a hill. To the right, below the red demon, a man is springing forward as if to strike at her,[2] while she points her finger at him. Above and beside her are some birds, one falling towards the hand of the man.

---

[1] This figure is very perfect and deserves copying.

[2] His head and shoulders were cut out on 8th March 1879 by the Pêskar of Ajanta to present to a visitor.

On the gate to the left, a long-necked bird sits on the roof, and inside another bird pecks as if at food.

The man just mentioned appears to be on the roof of a building, to which he has reached by means of a ladder, seen a little to the right, leading down to the area below, and beside which a man with a long sword appears and probably is mounting. Is he the same as shown above ? In the palace below is an empty *gâdi* or *âsana*. To the right of the throne a woman in rich garniture sits and to the right a man also richly dressed sits upon a seat : both seem to be in grief. About half a dozen persons sit behind these, one fully dressed and holding a rod, may be the porter, and one has a sword and shield.

To the right, several more pieces have been cut out of the plaster which destroys the intelligibility of this picture.

To the right of the gateway already mentioned, a man is seated, richly jewelled ; another sat near him on the right but has been mostly peeled off. Behind the first, three soldiers stand, two with straight swords and oblong shields chequered in different patterns, apparently bent over, and green on the inner-sides —the middle soldier with the crooked Nepalese weapon. To the right a head only is left. Behind the soldiers are two horses, and a red-skinned man stands holding them. Below this a râja was represented on a seat (but the Peśkar has cut him out). Beside him a jewelled figure sits, and behind, to the right, a red man. Below, in front of the râja, sat another figure looking at him and holding up his left hand as if speaking, perhaps about the man and demon to the left. A soldier with a sword in his hand, standing on his right, looks up in that direction. To the right sits a man with a string of pearls, looking also to the left. Further to the right stand three more soldiers with chequered shields, Nepalese swords, and small *dhôtîs*, with long trains and abundant hair tied up with a ribbon.

XLIV.

Above, and to the right of the building containing the Râkshasîs, were two figures seated on an *âsana* with five others on the ground in front facing them. Below these are two soldiers talking together and others standing by.

XLV.

Above the cell door the plaster is a good deal destroyed. A palace has been represented, and a banner with three pennants from it on the left. To the right a râja on his elephant, with the driver on its neck and an attendant behind, are proceeding to the right. Before him go some soldiers two with long spears. Below, to the right, is a horse, and in front of it, is a seat under which is a human face, and to the right some royal personage with the umbrella carried over the head. Still to the right, in a dwelling, a man richly be-jewelled sits on a seat, and in front of him an old man stands leaning upon a stick—dressed in the complete clothing of a porter.

To the right of this the painting is blackened by smoke, but a main part of this picture comes in just below, where a man in rich striped dress holds two horses, while in front of them stands a man supplicating the seated one above. The supplicant is in a rich and variegated dress, with a splendid dark coloured scarf falling over his right shoulder : he is either slightly bald or has a flower on his hair, and wears a long straight sword. To the right is another less richly dressed, but also with sword, and in the attitude of supplication. Another kneels behind, and then another square piece has been cut out of the plaster just above. Five other soldiers stand to the right, in front of the horses, some also in variegated dresses, and beyond the horses is seen a head. It may be that this is some deputation to a râja connected with the picture below.

XLVI.

Taking now the lower portion of the great picture between the doors of the second and third cells :—On the extreme left, a râja, shadowed by an umbrella, wearing his crown, and on his great white elephant, comes out from a gateway, hedged about with spears, some bearing pennants. A light coloured elephant is on his left and a reddish one on his right, and each rider has a sheaf of arrows by the flank of his elephant. The red and white elephants have intertwined their trunks. Six soldiers with sword and shield march along side them (see plate XIX).

Below, four mounted soldiers are seen in a boat, with spears, and in front of them, to the right, are again represented the three elephants, also in boats, with their riders, &c., all with umbrellas as before—but engaged in battle—the râja has just shot his arrow, and others in the back ground from among the spears and standards, are throwing spears and the discus. Some have landed and are pressing the battle from the shore. The enemies have long flowing fair hair, fair skins, and charge with the spear, but they are all females—Râkshasîs. One breaks a spear and others charge. Below, some of them realizing how unequal the contest is, are supplicating the râja. Above are the pyramidal hills of the invaded country.

Above the right side of this picture, is a Râja enthroned, and two men pouring on him the *abhisheka*. His eyes, have a stony glare, unlike most others, and it may be suggested whether they were not originally put in of gold leaf or other material, over the white paint, which alone is now left. To the right and left are *châmara*-bearers ; in front to the left, are three men with cymbals and two with drums ; on the right, one stands with clothing over his arm, another beside him, and two more with drums. Mrs. Speir is probably correct in supposing that this represents the landing and coronation of Vijaya in Ceylon.[1]

XLVII.

Above the cell door, almost the only figure that can be made out, is a white Râkshasî, seated ; her legs apart, and apparently asleep with a cup in her hand. To the right sits another, and beside her a red-skinned man, part of whose entrails seem torn out by her, and which she is devouring. He sits, however, quite unconcernedly. Still to the right, are a third and fourth Râkshasî, both with long crooked knives, and the lower one holding a man by the throat, about to dissect him. Below is a fifth, holding the crooked knife in her right hand, over the body of a man whose breast has been slit open, while with the left she quaffs a cup of gore.

To the right of this is a house with a pyramidal roof in which sit a man and his wife, the man with a cup in his hand.

Below this last, most of the plaster for some distance is destroyed, but on a fragment that is left, are portions of the heads of two well drawn richly jewelled ladies.

---

[1] *Life in Ancient India*, pp. 300 to 302, Plate XIX is an enlarged photolithograph from Mrs. Speir's book, p. 303.

XLVIII.

At the bottom of the panel, between the doors of the first and second cells, are painted two boats, each with three masts, in the sea, and in several places are pieces of coral, a large fish in front of the left hand boat, and below it a still larger one.

In the right hand boat, the left mast is finished off with a trident (*triśula*). Beyond it is a man holding a rope from the other boat and apparently about to get in, beside him is the head of a sea monster, somewhat like a boar. To the right of it is seen, over the boat, another man's head, and still to the right a third, while further behind are other two and a green-skinned man holding the prow of the left hand boat as if pushing it back. In it is seen a big red-skinned man, holding up his hands, and to the left, a fair one holding a pole, but whether to push off the boat or one of two red men in the water in front of it, is not clear. One of these comes out of the mouth of a *makara*. Another red-skinned one is in the water behind, just in front of the largest fish. Below him is another white-skinned person near some shrubs.

XLIX[1].

To the right of the roof of the house, above No. 47, are five women, one standing with a child in her arms, while they mostly look towards a man flying up to the left.

There are figures seated above, mostly red-skinned, but too much smoked to be made out without careful dusting and varnishing.

L.

To the right of No. 49, in an interior, sit a great man—pale-skinned—and his ruddy wife, their hair in fillets; the wife offers him a cup, while his cloth is carried round the right knee to give him support (*palavatiyuṅ*). In the next apartment to the right, a similar (or the same) pair are seated, she passing her hand across in front of him and up by his right ear.

Below the left part a *Râkshasî*, with boar tusks, but otherwise comely and richly jewelled, sleeps on a bed, with large chignon tied about with a ribbon. At her head is perhaps a casket. In front of her legs a man with but little clothing sits, and beyond, her a lady stands with a vessel or casket in her hand—perhaps carrying it off—her husband holding out his hand for it. In front of the bed-stead sits another woman.

To the right of these, and just over the cell-door, a woman in green *chôlî* and striped *saḍî* seems to be swinging herself on a sort of ladder.

LI.

On the upper part of the front of the pilaster is a lady and two female attendants, one with *châmara*, and the other with a tray on which is a classically formed casket and other things for the toilet.

LII.

Below No. 51 is a Râja with two servants and a dwarf.

---

[1] Nos. 47, 49, 50 should be preserved if possible.

LIII.

The right end of the front aisle is unfortunately much damaged by bats and nest-building insects,[1] but perhaps as interesting as any portion of this cave, and if only saved now, before the destruction is complete, it might be of real service to science.

The upper portion to the left of the cell door presents a râja and his retinue coming from the hills, riding on his elephant which he drives with the *ankuśa* himself, with a man in green clothing carrying the umbrella over him with sword and dagger, who is prevented from falling off by a rope fastened to the seat and passing round his waist. On each side, also on elephants, ride persons of distinction. Banners of various devices on spears precede and follow him, and above is a drum in the clouds, beaten by some *gandharva*.

Two horses precede, and two soldiers—one beating a drum and the other with a spear who seems to be shouting. By the side of the râja are two more—one with shield and sword, and one with spear and shield, and behind them a man carries a *bhangi*. On the extreme right is a small hill; and above are some figures, which careful varnishing may bring out.

Over the cell door is a gate way. Under a canopy to the right with a small cloth fringe, a number of Bhikâris appear, who have just come in; one has a square umbrella over his shoulder, and all proceed to a lofty wooden erection. To it they seem to have come begging, and before it a man and woman have sat down, each with a small black dish in which they seem to have received some alms from a man who comes from the house with a *kumbha* or earthen vessel in his hands. Behind him is a green female also with a vessel on her left hand. In front a *bhikâri* sits and drinks out of black bowl or dish; and to the right a man comes in with a large open vessel on his shoulder. To the right of these is a hill.

LIV.

Below, on the left of the cell door and on the return of the pilaster, we have the story of Śibi Râja. On the pilaster, under a tree, sit two râja-like persons, both with crowns and much jewellery, the one on the right a little above, and Śibi on the left. Below is a pond and *kamala* flowers, and behind—a hill.

On the end wall, we have Śibi Râja again seated on an *âsana* and the name below him. To the right sit two young men with jewellery, one apparently speaking and the other with his hands joined.

Below sits one with jewelled head-dress resting on one hand and looking up excitedly. Behind him to the right a man stands with a dish, on the extreme

---

[1] On the injury done to these paintings by bats and nest-building insects, Mr. Griffiths very pertinently remarks. "What would be the effect if a few hundred of them were allowed to flutter over Michael Angelo's fresco on the ceiling of the Sistine Chapel, or among the paintings of the greatest of the Venetians in the Camera di Collegio in the Ducal Palace? I had daily opportunity, for nearly six months, for watching their movements; and I am fully convinced that they have been one of the principal agents in hastening the destruction of the paintings. They glide along the surface of the wall, or cling to the ceiling by their sharp claws, removing loose particles of stucco; their urine, mixing with the dust, runs down the walls in long streaks, forming a black, slimy, fetid mess.

"The mason bees have built their innumerable mud cells over wall and ceiling; and when I have had occasion to remove some of the cells to get at the painting underneath, I have found it extremely difficult to do so without destroying the painting, owing to their hardness and the tenacity with which they adhere to the stucco."—*Report for 1872-73, p. 11.*

right an elephant, and in the background are two attendants. Before the râja, in the foreground, is a red attendant, and behind him, to the right, is seen the head of a richly jewelled lady and the hilt of the state sword, and at his left sits perhaps his rânî. Above, a râja-like figure comes flying with high *mukuṭa*, and the name 'Indra' written at the side of it, and again a head like his is shown on the left of the Rânî.[1]

Continuing the story on the right of the cell-door, we have the râja on his *gâdi*, resting against a pillow, with his right hand on the front of the seat, and the left upon his eye, and beneath is written Śibi Râja. To the right sits a lady with her left hand on her breast, and right raised as if forbidding something and looking excitedly across to the left. Behind her a woman presses a cloth to her face as if crying.

On the left of the râja sits a man in rich dress (perhaps Siwaka) with a fillet about his hair, and not looking well pleased and apparently speaking to the râja. Behind him an old man (like a beggar) stands addressing or asking something of the Râja and *Indrah* written on his waist. Behind are seen an ox and a horse.

LV.

On the front wall, between the end of the front aisle and the first window, is a scene in good preservation, in which the figures generally differ from those elsewhere, in that, with few exceptions, they are clothed from the neck to the toes.

A great man on the extreme, left with the umbrella over his head, goes out a hunting on horseback, with another before him also on horseback, carrying a bow and his hair in a fillet. To the right the first rider has alighted and places his hand in that of another whom he meets, while the horse-keeper holds the horse, and in the foreground, a red man, not so fully clothed, points to a deer on the right, and another behind it; above to the right a lion or tiger is seen in its den. Above all this is a râja on a tall white horse with the umbrella over

---

[1] The following is Gogerby's version of the *Jâtaka* of S'ibi Râja :—

"I was S'ibi, king of the city of the Aritha, and sitting in my magnificent palace, I thus thought —There is no kind of alms among men which I have not given, if any one should even beg from me my eyes, I would give them without hesitation.

"S'akra, the Sovereign of the gods, knew my thoughts, and sitting amidst his attendant gods he thus spoke. The king S'ibi, possessing super-human power, sitting in his magnificent palace, and meditating on the various kinds of alms, does not perceive one that he has not given. I will ascertain what his thoughts are; wait here a moment until I know his mind. Having assumed the form of a trembling, hoary-headed, wrinkled, decayed and emaciated blind man, he approached the king. He having assumed this form, elevating his left and his right arms, with clasped hands raised to his head, he spake these words. Great and just sovereign, the author of your kingdom's prosperity, the fame of your alms-giving has ascended up to gods and men; I have a petition. I am become blind of both eyes give me one of your eyes and retain the other for your own use.

"When I had heard these words, with a mind excited by joyful emotions, I thus addressed the trembling supplicant—Thou who hast come soliciting the gift of an eye hast come knowing my thoughts while I was in the palace. My desires are accomplished, my wish is fulfilled. I shall this day give a suppliant such alms as I never gave before. Come here Siwaka : arise, be not unskilful, be not negligent, pluck out both my eyes and give to the beggar. My obedient slave Siwaka being thus addressed, plucked out my eyes like the kernels of a palm-tree and gave them to the beggar.

"In purposing to give, in giving, and after having given the alms, I had no other design than that of becoming a Buddha. Not that I had an aversion to my two eyes, my body was not disagreeable to me; but my desire was to become a Buddha, and therefore I gave my eyes"—*Jour. Ceylon, Br. R. As. Soc., vol. II., pp.* 5, 6.

his head and quiver by his thigh, and behind him two elephants, while in the background to the right are three more horses and riders, and in the foreground, to the right, seven attendants, three of them with swords, one going by the horse, one with bow and quiver, one with a *bhangi*, and one playing some fife or wind instrument; they are attended by several dogs, very badly drawn; while on the entreme right is a great *rath* or car, on which is a deer.

This extends about half way up the window jamb. The painting is continued up to the roof, but so blackened as not to be made out unless it can be cleaned.

LVI.

Between the windows are some fragments, among which may be made out an archer drawing his bow and his quiver at his back; some figures above; and a dahgoba near the ceiling. On a tree above the second window from the end, are a number of birds and some deer.

Between this last window and the door, a good deal of painting remains, sadly defaced below by the villainous conduct of some person who has been paring off the plaster with a knife. To the extreme right, in a palace, a râja sits, to the left his rânî, behind stand three *dâsîs*, and in front two men sit. On the left, a Brâhman or beggar, without jewels, sits on a stool. A woman stands in the door and looks out towards a man who kneels in front of the steps and talks to her.

To the left is a râja with *mukuṭa*, *chhatra*, and with him the man who was kneeling at the door, and attendants. They approach the door of another house, in which is a spotted deer and a man who speaks to the approaching râja. To the left is a kitchen in which lies a large spotted deer, and one man sits looking at it, with two standing behind him, while one pushes a stick into a fire on which are several large pots.

Above, between the two buildings, is a canopy in which is a seat (*âsana*) and a râja seated beside it, with several attendants with him.

LVII.

Below, much has been pared off, but to the left, near a hill, a horseman is seen and another figure before him, while in the background, monkeys are amusing themselves in front of the roof of a gateway. Farther to the left is a horse's head and that of a man with a peculiar peaked head-dress and umbrella.

Still to the left is mountain scenery and several deer with young ones, some standing, some lying.

LVIII.

On the left side of the entrance is an interior scene, in which a râja, without jewels, appears on the left, seated on a long couch, with two pillows behind him, and with him a young female—his rânî—wearing a kirtle, on his lap, whom he appears to support. Just beyond is a female with the hair done up in a *jaṭâ* and with a receding forehead and long nose, speaking to the râja; chafing or rubbing the rânî's foot is a *dâsî*. Behind her to the right sits one with a breastband (*sthanapati*). Behind the râja a female stands with a necklace and a *châmara*; besides her, one with a feather-fan; and next to her a bald-headed eunuch, in full white dress. On the right a man in white clothing brings in a basket with something in it, and in the background another shaven-headed man with a rod talks to the eunuch (*kanchukî*).

LIX.

Below, the plaster is much broken, but there has been a representation of a pond with lotos (*kamala*) flowers in it, and elephants breaking off the flowers,—one a very large white one. To the right is a high mountain with trees, up which go a man and woman, he having a sword in his belt and bow and an arrow in his hand. The woman rests her left hand on his shoulder, and is dressed in thinnest gauze with a *mekhalâ* or waistband of jewels, armlets, and her hair done up with flowers.

In front of them is a monkey and three *chakrawâkas*. Below, some wild animal has sprung upon the back of an elephant. Above is a very large white elephant, without housings. In front of it are two men both with swords in their waistbands and bows: one looks round at the elephant, and the other makes obeisance to it. Above to the left are other elephants and a man who has got up to the corner of the râja's mansion, and looking in, seems to say something.

LX.

Above the window are two figures in white. Between the window and side door the whole of the plaster is too much damaged to make anything out except a large light-coloured horse.

LXI.

Between the window and the left end of the aisle, an elephant kneels, and beyond it is a figure like Buddha, with another to the right and four to the left. Below is a mountain and five men in the foreground.

The whole of the pillars have been painted with every variety of decorative device and many of them are even yet in a state that, with a little care, might be copied.

CAVE XVIII.

Cave XVIII is merely a porch, 19 feet 4 inches by 8 feet 10 inches with two pillars, apparently intended as part of a passage into the next cave and possibly also to cover a water cistern.

CAVE XIX.

Cave XIX is the third of the *Chaitya* Caves, and differs only in its details from Nos. IX. and X. It is 24 feet wide by 46 feet long and 24 feet 4 inches high. But, whereas the former two were almost perfectly plain, this is elaborately carved throughout. Besides the two in front, the nave has fifteen columns, 11 feet high. These pillars are square at the base, which is 2 feet 7 inches high, with small figures on the corners; then they have an octagonal belt, about a foot broad, above which the shaft is circular, and has two belts of elaborate tracery, the intervals being in some cases plain and in others fluted with perpendicular or spiral flutes; above the shaft is a deep torus of slight projection between two fillets, wrought with a leaf-pattern, and over this again, is a square tile, supporting a bracket capital richly sculptured with a Buddha in the centre and elephants, or *śârdûlas* with two riders, or flying figures, on the bracket wings. The architrave consists of two plain narrow fascias. The whole entablature is 5 feet deep, and the frieze, occupying exactly the same position as the triforium would, in a Christian church, is divided into compartments by rich bands of arabeque, and in the compartments are figures of Buddha—alternately sitting cross-legged and standing. The roof rises 8 feet 4 inches over this, whilst the width of the nave is only 12 feet 2 inches so that the arch is higher than a semicircle, and is ribbed in stone. Between the feet of every fourth and fifth rib there is carved a tiger's head.

The *Chaitya* or *dahgoba*—which represents a monument raised to enshrine the relics of Buddha or of some *arhat* or Buddhist saint is a composite one; it has a low pedestal, on the front of which stand two demi-columns, supporting an arch containing a *basso-rilievo* figure of Buddha; on the under part of the *tee* or capital above the dome, there is also a small sculpture of Buddha, and over the *churamani* or four fillets of the capital, are three umbrellas, in stone, one above another, each upheld on four sides by small figures. These may be symbolic of Buddha—"the bearer of the triple canopy—the canopy of the heavenly host, the canopy of mortals, and the canopy of eternal emancipation," or they are typical of the *Bhuvanas* or heavens of the celestial Bodhisatvas and Buddhas.

The roof of the aisles is flat, and has been painted, chiefly with ornamental flower scrolls, Buddhas and *Chaityas*; and on the walls there have been paintings of Buddha—generally with attendants, the upper two rows sitting, and in the third mostly standing, but all with aureoles behind the heads.

There is but one entrance to this cave. The whole is in excellent preservation, as is also the façade, and as Mr. Fergusson remarks, "very little labour would free the lower part from the accumulated materials, and display entire one of the most perfect specimens of Buddhist art in India." The porch and whole front of the cave are covered with the most elaborate and beautiful carving, which it is impossible to describe in detail.[1]

Outside to the left, and at right angles to the façade of the cave, is a sculpture, representing a Nâga Râja, sitting under the expanded hoods of a seven-headed cobra and his wife with a single hood. To the left stands a female *chauri*-bearer, also with a single snake-hood. This probably represents some royal patron of Buddhism—perhaps some Nâga king. But who the Nâgas really were is still problematical. They were probably aborigines of the Dekhan, and may have left a trace of their name in 'Nâgpur.'

On the other side is a porch with two pillars and pilasters in front, which Mr. Fergusson supposes, and probably correctly, was a *chávadi* or place of rest for pilgrims. It has a room at each end, about 10 feet by 8 feet 4 inches. The capitals of the pillars in front of it are richly wrought with bunches of mangoes at the corners, and of grapes, (or the custard-apple), in the middle of the capitals. On the right of the main entrance is a sculpture of Buddha with his alms-bowl and a woman pushing her little boy forward to put something into it. This is the same scene as is painted on the left of the shrine-door of Cave XVII.

On each side the great arch is a large figure in rich head-dress;—that on the left is Kubéra—the god of wealth—a great favourite with the Buddhists (as with many who are not). The figure on the right is very nearly the same. Many Buddhas sitting or standing occupy compartments in the façade and at the sides of it.

---

[1] See wood-cut in Fergusson's *Hist. of East Architecture*, p. 125.

Over the whole façade of this Chaitya temple projects a bold and carefully carved cornice,—broken only at the left end by a heavy mass of rock having given way. In front has been an enclosed court, 33 feet wide by 30 feet deep, but the left side of it has nearly disappeared.

The style of ornamentation on the pillars and other parts of this cave so strongly resemble those of No. I as to render it very probable that they were excavated about the same age,—not likely before the middle of the sixth century.

The Painting in Cave XIX.

This cave contains many painted Buddhas in the aisles and a few others with figures of Chaityas still remain in the roof. The roof of the front aisle contains some exquisite panels, and those of the side aisles are painted in a rich-floriated pattern.

In the chapel to the right of the front are some fragments of painting, especially on the roof.

CAVE XX.

Cave XX. is a small Vihâra with two pillars and two pilasters in front of its verandah. One pillar is broken, but on each side of the capitals there is a pretty statuette of a female under a canopy of foliage. The roof of the verandah is hewn in imitation of beams and rafters. There is a cell at each end of the verandah and two on each side of the hall,—which is 28 feet 2 inches wide by 25 feet 4 inches deep, and 12½ feet high, and has no columns. The roof is supported by the walls and front of the antechamber, which advances 7 feet into the cave, and has in front two columns in antis, surmounted by a carved entablature filled with seven figures of Buddha and attendants. On the sides below are a *Nâga dwârapâla;* then a man and his wife with a *pankhâwâlî* and another attendant; and above, a tall female standing on a *makara* under foliage, with an attendant. The attendant on the right side is a male standing on a tortoise. Behind, on the left, is Buddha and attendants in a niche. The statue in the shrine was known to the Bhills as Matsyendranath. It has probably been painted red, and is attended by two large figures of Indras, each with some round object (a cocoanut ?) in his left hand, with great tiaras, and bearing *chaurts*; while on the front of the seat, which has no lions at the corners, are carved two deer as *vâhana*, with a *chakra* between them. The ornamentations over the cell-doors remind one of the similar carving at Ghatoṭkachh.

Painting in Cave XX.

Bits of the roof decoration and its general pattern can be made out, but the wall-paintings have all disappeared, only small fragments of the plaster remaining to show that this cave was all painted at one time.

CAVE XXI.

From the last cave we pass on for a considerable distance along the face of the scarp to No. XXI. Its verandah has fallen away, but the elaborately-carved pilasters at each end, in the style of Cave I, indicate that it was probably finished with the same richness of ornamentation. At each end is a neat open chapel like those in Caves I and II. The hall is 51½ feet wide by 51 feet deep, and has chapels with pillared fronts in the middle and at the back ends of the side aisles,—each leading into an inner cell; and besides these there are four other cells in each side wall. The fronts of the chapels in the back wall are surmounted by friezes with some good carving and devices.

The roof of the hall is supported by twelve columns, ornamented in a style similar to those in Cave II. The entrance to the adytum is unfinished, and the image sits cross-legged in the *dharma-chakra mudrâ*, has long ears, and is attended by *chaurî*-bearers—the right side one unfinished below—with high, ornate tiaras, and perhaps represent Indras. Above are *Vidyâdharas*.

The Painting in Cave XXI.

Large pieces of the roof painting in the front and back aisles are still pretty distinct, the blues being as fresh as they were a thousand years ago; geometrical patterns having a preponderance. The soffits of the brackets are decorated with two bands of brick-red with flowers in them in white and brown.

Of the roof of the central hall a portion of painting is still left, but scarcely more than the pattern,—the colours having peeled off or faded.

On the left wall are a few figures of Buddha and to the left of them two very fair female figures.

Probably the walls of this cave never were all painted; portions of smooth plaster remain apparently never touched by the brush.

CAVE XXII.

The next is a very small Vihâra, about 16½ feet square and 9 feet high, with four unfinished cells, no window, a very pretty door, and a narrow verandah, of which both the pillars are broken,—ascended to by two steps. The sanctuary opens directly from the cave, and contains an image with its feet on the lotos, the Buddhist emblem of creative power. On front of the *sinhasana* or seat is the *chakra*—the *chinha* or cognisance of Sâkya, with two small deer as *vâhana* or supporters, and worshippers on each side. The *chaurî*-bearer on the left is Padmapâni, and on the right is another attendant with curled hair—perhaps Indra.

On the right side, below the painting and inscriptions, is a sculpture of Buddha squatted on the lotos with *chaurî*-bearers, and above his head two little *devas* holding up a crown. On the other side of the shrine a pair of standing figures are only roughly blocked out.

Painting in Cave XXII.

A fragment on the roof at each end of the back wall has been painted; and on the right side a piece on the back wall and a little on the right side wall near the back, with three figures of Buddha on the lower portion of it.

On the upper part of the wall on the right side of the shrine are seven painted Buddhas, each under his Bodhi tree and their names painted beneath,—

Vipaśvi. Śikhi. Visvabhu...Kanakhamuni. Kaśyapa. Śákya-Múni. Maitreya. The missing name being Krakuchanda or Kakusanda, the first Buddha of the present Kalpa or regeneration of the world; for the Buddhists believe that the world is destroyed and regenerated at the end of immensely long periods or Kalpas; and that each Kalpa has one or more Buddhas;—

thus in the third past regeneration, Vipaśvi was the Buddha, in the last Śikhi and Visvabhu; and in the present Krakuchanda, Kanakamuni, Kaśyapa, and Śákya Mûni or Gautama, have already appeared as Buddhas, whilst Arya Maitreya, the last, is yet to come five thousand years after Śákya. These are also known as the *manushya* or earth-born Buddhas. Below these names is painted in one line, an inscription, which reads,—

"The charitable assignation of S'ákhya Bhikshu...May the merit of this...be to father and mother and to all beings...endowed with beauty and good fortune, good qualities and organs, the bright...protectors of light...thus become pleasing to the eye."

CAVE XXIII.

This is another twelve-pillared Vihâra, 50 feet 5 inches wide by 51 feet 8 inches deep and 12 feet 4 inches high. The four columns of the verandah are almost perfect. They have bases, 2¾ to 3 feet square; the shafts are circular, the end ones fluted,—and on the torus of the capital are four dwarfs, upholding the corners of a square abacus or tile under the brackets. The door has small *dwârapâlas*, canopied by the many-hooded snake. There are chapels at the ends of the verandah and of the left aisle, but the sanctuary is only commenced.

There is no trace of painting in this cave.

CAVE XXIV.

Cave XXIV is quite unfinished, but was evidently intended for a large Vihâra, 73¼ feet wide and 75 feet deep, with twenty pillars, and, if completed, would probably have been one of the most beautiful in the whole series. The verandah was long choked up with earth, and of its six pillars only one is now standing; the rest appear to have fallen down within the last thirty years. The bracket capitals still hang from the entablature, and the carved groups on them are in the best style of workmanship. In two of the capitals and in those of the chapels at the end of the verandah, the corners are left above the torus, and wrought into pendant scroll leaf ornaments. The work on the doors and windows is elaborate. Inside, only one column has been finished.

Here we learn how these caves were excavated by working long alleys with the pick-axe into the rock and then breaking down the intervening walls except where required for supporting columns. There is some sculpture in an inner apartment of the chapel outside the verandah to the left, but much in the usual style.

CAVE XXV.

This is a small Vihâra higher up in the rock, with a verandah of two pillars; the hall is 26 feet 5 inches wide by 25 feet 4 inches deep without cell or sanctuary. It has three doors; and at the left end of the verandah is a chamber with cells at the right and back. In front is an en closed space, about 30¼ feet by 14, with two openings in front, and a door to the left leading on to the terrace of the next cave.

CAVE XXVI.

This is the fourth Chaitya-cave, and bears a strong resemblance to Cave XIX. Its sculptures, if somewhat monotonous and in some few cases inferior in design and execution, are far more numerous and more elaborate than in any other cave of the series. The work may belong to about the middle of the sixth century of our era. It once had a verandah along the whole front, supported by four columns, of which, portions of three still remain, and at each end of the varandah there was a chamber with two pillars and pilasters very like those in the left side chapel of Cave III at Aurangâbâd. The Court outside the verandah has extended some way right and left, and on the right side are two panels above one another containing the litany of Avalokitêśvara, similar to that in Cave IV., and to the right of it is a standing figure of Buddha in the *aśiva mudrâ*,—holding up the right hand—in the attitude of blessing. One of these panels, however, is much hidden by the accumulation of earth in front of them, and the other is entirely concealed by it. Over the verandah, in front of the great window and upper façade of the cave, here was a balcony, about 8¼ feet wide and 40 feet long, entered at the end from the front of the last cave. The sill of the great arch was raised 2¾ feet above this, and at the inner side of the sill, which is 7 feet 2 inches deep, there is a stone parapet or screen, 3¾ feet high, carved in front with small Buddhas. The outer arch is 14¼ feet high, but the inner one from the top of the screen is only 8 feet 10 inches. The whole façade outside the great arch, and the projecting side-walls at the ends of the balcony, have been divided into compartments of various sizes sculptured with Buddhas. On each side the great arch is a seated figure of Kubêra, and beyond it, in a projecting alcove, is a standing Buddha. On the upper parts of the end walls of this terrace there is, on each side, a figure of Buddha standing with his *śelâ* or robe descending from the left shoulder to the ankle, leaving the right shoulder bare: these figures are about 16 feet high. Under the one on the left is an inscription (plate XXI) in two lines, reading thus,—

[१] देयधर्म्मोयंशाक्य भिक्षोर्भदन्तगुणाकरस्य यदत्र पुण्यं तद्भवतु मातापितरं पुर्व्वङ्गमं कि (कृ) त्वा

[२] सर्व्व सत्वेभ्य अनुत्तर ज्ञाना वाप्तये.

The projecting cornice above is unfortunately almost entirely broken off.

There is an inscription, on the left of the front of this cave, which was translated by Dr. Bhau Dâji. It contains but little historical data, being merely a string of praises of the Sugatas or Buddhists and of Bhavvirâja, the minister of Asmakarâja, and of his son Dêvarâja, who constructed the temple. It has been transliterated anew by Bhagvanlâl Indraji, and runs thus:—

(१) जयति लोकहिताबहितोद्यतो–हिसुखान्तकरः परमार्थवित् त्रिविधनिर्म्मलसर्वगुणोदयो मु [षितमी : ?] करुणामलचन्द्रिकः

(२) पुनरपि[1]मरणादि येन सम्यक्षिवमजरामरधर्म्मता च लब्धा शिवमभयमनन्तमाक्षयं गतोपि प्रशमपुरं जगतां करोति चार्त्थं

(३) ततो नमस्कारगुणाभिधानं भवत्यवन्ध्यं विपुलं महार्थं प्रवृत्तमेकं कुसुमं च यत्र स्वर्गापवर्गा ख्यफलस्य हेतुः

(४) अत इह विदुषा तथागतेषु प्रथितगुणाधिकलोकवत्सलेषु कृतमनुसरता जनेन कार्य्या इयक हणाहृदयेष्वती

(५) बभक्तिः देवा निरस्तविजयास्सविपत्तिकत्वाच्छापेन शंभुरपि काचरलोचनो भूत् कृष्णो वशोपि वशमापतितोन्तकस्य तस्माज्जयन्ति

[1] Read वि.

(६) सुगता भयविप्रमुक्ताः स्थविराचलेन मुनिना शासनमुद्भावयकृ[2]तज्ञन क्रितकृ[3]त्येनापि स त
शैलगृहं कारितं शास्तुः

(७) प्रागेव बोधिसत्वैर्भवसुखकामैश्च मोक्षकामैश्च संविद्यमानविभवैः कथम्न काय्र्या भवेत्कीर्तिः
यावत्कीर्तिर्ल्लोके तावत्स्वर्गे

(८) मुमोदति च देही चन्द्रार्क्ककालकल्पा काय्र्या कीर्तिर्म्महीध्रेषु अनेकजन्मांतरबद्धसौहृदं स्थिरं-
कृतज्ञं सुधियं विपाश्चितम्

(९) सुरासुराचार्यमतेषु कोविदं महानुभावाश्मकरानमंत्रिणम् लोकज्ञमेकान्तसमन्तभद्रं सर्व्वार्या
नामर्थकरं सुवाचं गुणोन्नतं प्रश्रय

(१०) नम्रमूर्तिं ख्यातिं गतं सच्चरितैः पृथिव्यां दण्डसाध्यानि कार्याणि न्यायाभिकरसान्यपि य
स्साधयति साम्नैव नृपतेर्म्मन्त्रिपुङ्गवः इत्थं

(११) भूतोस्य पुत्रोपि देवराजो धुरन्धरः पितर्य्युपरते येन पदमुन्नामितं गुणैः तं भव्विराजमुद्दि
श्य मातापितरमेवच भिक्षुणा बुद्धभद्रेण

(१२) कारितः सुगतालयः आगम्य धर्म्मदत्तञ्च भिक्षुं सच्छिष्यमेव च भद्रबन्धुमिदं वेश्म ताभ्य
निष्पादितं च मे यदत्र पुण्यं तत्तेषां

(१३) जगतां च भवत्विदं सर्व्वामलगुणख्यातमहाबोधि फलाप्तये यो बुद्धशासनगतिं समबुध्य
जातो भिक्षुर्व्वयस्यभिनवे भिननोपपन्नः

(१४) बहुव्रतः शीलविशुद्धचेता लोकस्य मोक्षाय कृताधिकारः न संसारापन्नं शुभमपितु किञ्च
च्छुभकरं विपाकी दिव्यो

(१५) —य —- - चनियमा - - - लोकात्थाय प्रसृत - - - पुण्यमहतां विपाको धीराण
भवति सुखभोगाय

(१६) जगताम् - - - - - बलभिर्मानाण्डनव्याहते गोलाङ्गूलनिनादपूरितदरे प्राग्भावि -
—- - -

(१७) योगीश्वराध्यासिते वेश्मेदं न - — - जनकभूत्वे प्रतिष्ठापितं पूर्व्वाऽपिचेयं तेनैव त्रिकधा-
चार्येण सौगतिम् लोकचिन्तामुपादाय - - - - - - - - - - - - - - - - - -

Besides the central door, there is a smaller side one into each aisle. The temple is 67 feet 10 inches deep, 36 feet 3 inches wide, and 31 feet 3 inches high. The nave—besides the two in front, has twenty-six columns, is 17 feet 7 inches wide, and 33 feet 8 inches long to the front of the *Chaitya*; the pillars behind the dahgoba are plain octagons, with bracket capitals, and the others somewhat resemble those in the verandah of Cave II, they are 12 feet high, and a four-armed bracket dwarf is placed over each capital on the front of the narrow architrave. The frieze projects a few inches over the architrave, and is divided into compartments elaborately sculptured. The stone ribs of the roof project inwards, and the vault rises 12¾ feet to the ridge pole.

---

[2] Read क्व.   [3] Read कृ.

The body of the *Chaitya* or *Dahgoba* is cylindrical, but a broad face has been left on the front, carved with pilasters, cornice, and maṇḍapa top, and in the centre is a Buddha sitting on a *siñhâsana* or throne with lions upholding the seat, his *śelâ* reaching to his ankles, his feet on a lotos upheld by two small figures with *Nâga* canopies, behind which, and under the lions, are two elephants. The rest of the cylinder is divided by pilasters into compartments containing figures of Buddha standing in various attitudes. The dome has a compressed appearance, its greatest diameter being at about a third of its height, and the representation of the box above is figured on the sides with a row of standing and another of sitting Buddhas; over it are some eight projecting fillets or tænias, crowned by a fragment of a small stone umbrella. The aisles of this Chaitya contain a good deal of sculpture, much of it defaced. In the right aisle there are large compartments with Buddhas sculptured in *alto-rilievo*, with attendants; their feet rest on the lotos upheld by *Nâga*-protected figures with rich head-dresses, and others sitting beside them. Over the Buddhas are flying figures, and above them a line of arabesques with small compartments containing groups.

On the left wall, near the small door, is a gigantic figure of Buddha about 23 feet 3 inches in length, reclining on a couch. This represents the death of the great ascetic. "It is," says Fahian, "to the north of Kusinara" (probably Kusia, between Betiya and Gorakhpur) "betwixt two *sâl* trees on the bank of the river Hiranyavati (probably the Gandak) that the 'Illustrious of the Age,' his face turned to the north, entered *nirvâṇa*. There where Subhadra long after obtained the law, and where they adored for seven days in his golden coffin the 'Illustrious of the Age;' there where 'the hero that bears the diamond sceptre' (Vajrapâni) let go the golden pestle, and where the eight kings divided the *sariro* (or relics), in all these places they established Sangharâmas or monasteries which exist to this day." The visitor will observe a tree at the head and another at the foot of the figure, and Ananda, the relative and attendant of Buddha, standing under the second. This figure has also its face turned to the north. "In a great chapel erected at Kusinara," says Hiwan Thsang—writing about A. D. 640—is a "representation of the *nirvâṇa* of the Tathâgata. His face is turned to the north, and hath the appearance of one slumbering."

Above the large figure are several very odd ones, perhaps representing the *dêvas* "making the air ring," as the legend says, "with celestial music, and scattering flowers and incense." Among them is perhaps Indra, the prince of the thirty-two *dêvas* of Trayastrinsha, on his elephant. In front of the couch are several other figures, his disciples or *bhikshus*, exhibiting their grief at his departure and a worshipper with a flower in his hand and some little offerings in a tray. Farther along the wall, beyond a figure of Buddha teaching between two attendants—a Bodhisattva on the left and perhaps Padmapâni on the right—there is a large and beautiful piece of sculpture that has perplexed every one who has attempted to explain it (Plate XX). It is the trial of Buddha by Mâra.[1] To the left a prince, Mâra, stands with what appears to be a bow and arrow in his hands and protected by an umbrella, and before him—some

---

[1] The following is a Sinhalese account of this scene:—

"The dêva Wasawartti-mâra reflected thus: 'This is the day on which Siddhârtha will become Buddha; but I must go and endeavour to prevent it, I have been trying for the space of six years to overcome him, but have not been able; if this opportunity be lost, no other will be presented.' He then struck the great drum called *Wasawartti-ghôsa*, and all the *Dêvas* and *Brahmas* on hearing its sound, trembled with fear and shut their eyes; but to the prince it was as the rolling of the *timbili* drum, struck in seasons of festivity. It was a sign to him that Mâra would come to do battle, and as he knew who would be the conqueror, and that by this means his prowess would be

sitting, others dancing, are a number of females, his daughters Tanhâ, Ratî, and Rangâ with richly-adorned head-dresses. A female beats three drums, two of which stand on end which she beats with one hand and the other lies on

---

proclaimed to the world, he sat in peace, undisturbed. When the retinue of Mâra heard the sound of the drum, they concluded that their lord was about to fight some battle, and therefore gathered around him, all carrying weapons. The *Dêva* mounted his elephant *Griměkhala*, 150 yojanas high; and as he knew that he would not be able to conquer with one weapon alone, he made unto himself 500 heads, with 1,000 red eyes, and 500 flaming tongues; he had also 1,000 arms, in each of which was a weapon, and yet no two of these weapons were alike. As he knew that the task he had undertaken would be difficult to accomplish, from the power and wisdom of his opponent, he concluded that it would be better not to approach him in front, lest he should be seen from afar, and the mind of the prince be prepared for the attack; it might be that if he approached from behind and made a noise, Siddhârtha would look to see what was the matter, which would be the proper moment in which to seize him. He therefore proceeded stealthily to the western side of the *sakwala-gala*. The army that accompanied him extended on every side 164 miles, and its weight was sufficient to overpoise the earth. No two of the warriors had the same appearance; they assumed the most frightful forms, appearing like lions, tigers, panthers, boars, bears, buffaloes, bulls, Nâgas, Garundas, Polongas, and Pimburas; all with hideous faces; the snakes stretched out their necks; other animals tore up trees by the roots; they rolled round their heads, struck each other as if in mortal combat, made mouths in the middle of their bodies, from which they put out their tongues and caused dirty saliva to exude, chased each other hither and thither, manifested various kinds of evil dispositions, brought terror upon all who saw them, and extended themselves from the *sakwala-gala* to the Bô-tree, without any intermediate vacancy.

When the *Dêvas* heard the noise of the army as it approached the tree, they all fled from the 1,000 *sakwalas*. Kalana who had come to dance in the presence of the prince, and sing hymns in his praise, accompanied by 60,000 Nâgas, descended 8,000 miles into the interior of the earth, to the Nâga-loka-Manjarika, on arriving at which, he covered his face with both hands, and cried out, 'Alas! the glory of Siddhârtha will this day be extinguished!' and having said this, he fell flat upon his couch, with his face downwards. Then the *S'akras* of the 10,000 *sakwalas* threw down the shells that they held in their hands, and fled away; but Sujampati, the S'akra of our own favoured *sakwala*, because he was born here, and had the power resulting from great merit, and was moreover very courageous, did not leave his place; nor did he throw down his shells; mounting to the summit of the *sakwala-gala*, he stood looking towards the Bô-tree. Thus also the Sujâma and Santusita dêvas of the 10,000 *sakwalas*, throwing down whatever they had in their hands, fled away. The Sahampati Mahâ-Brahmas of the 10,000 *sakwalas* fled away in like manner, after they had struck their umbrellas, like so many moons upon the summit of the *sakwala-gala*.

When the prince perceived that all the *dêvas* had fled, without any exception, he still remained unmoved as the rock Mahâ-Mêru, and fearless as the king of the lions when he sees a herd of elephants. Then seeing the army of Mâra coming towards him, he thought thus: 'This great army comes to fight against me alone; my parents are not here, no brother is with me, nor is any one else present to assist me, therefore the *pâramitâ* of Truth, that I have kept perfectly during four *asankyas* and a *kaplaksha* must be to me as a mother; the *pâramitâ* of Wisdom must be to me as a father; my knowledge of the *dharmma* must be to me as an assisting brother; my *pâramitâ* of kindness must be to me as most excellent friends, my firm faith must be to me as a beloved parent; my *pâramitâ* of patient-endurance must be to me as a helping son; these six relatives have continually preserved me until now, not leaving me for a single day or hour; therefore my relatives that are as my life are here: the thirty *pâramitâs* that I have kept continually until now, without any intermission, shall this day be as thirty warriors to protect me, and thus I have powerful defenders, the thirty-seven great virtues of the Buddhas are my nobles; the countless assemblage of my observances is as a powerful army. This powerful army of my observances will not leave to-day. My profound endowments will be to me as a deep fosse, my renowned benevolence will be to me as water filling it, and with this fosse around me the approach of my enemies shall be prevented. My *pâramitâs* shall be to me as bricks for the building of a strong wall, so high that it shall touch the *Brahma-lôka*; and this wall shall keep off my enemy Mâra when he approaches. The four great duties, *Chatuphari-sudhi-s'ila*, that I have constantly attended to, shall be as gates; the four observances of the senses *indrasangwara-s'ila* shall be as four trusty servants, who shall stand as wardens; and my wardens will not to-day open the gate to my enemies, but will protect me. This my throne shall be to me as the place of honour; this my illustrious Bô-tree shall be to me as a triumphal canopy and these two assistances, that have been produced by my own power, will not leave me to-day.' Thus the prince was encompassed by his *pâramitâs* as by a fortification; and by his obedience to the precepts as by a city surrounded with a wall and well defended; and he was therefore without fear.

At this moment Mâra came behind the tree, but he was not able to approach it, on account of the splendour proceeding from the body of Siddhârtha, so he caused a mighty wind to arise, that he

its side while she almost sits on it and beats it with the other hand. Mâra again sits at the right side, disappointed, at his failure. Several of the faces are beautifully cut. Above are his demon forces attacking the great ascetic sitting under

---

might hurl him into the next *sakwala;* and a violent wind it was, as it tore up rocks twenty or thirty miles in size, threw down great trees, and blew as at the end of a *kalpa;* yet as it went and came, not even a leaf of the tree was shaken; not even the corner of his rope was disturbed, nor was a single hair of his head at all moved; like a gentle and agreeable breese it refreshed him, did homage to him, and passed away. Then Mâra, that he might see into what *sakwala* the prince was blown by the storm, mounted to the top of the Udayagiri rock; but when he saw his body still resplendent as the orb of the sun, he became angry as a stricken serpent, and thought within himself, 'I will cause a thick rain to fall and destroy him by the force of the water'; intending to cause a rain like that which falls at the end of *kalpa.*

By his great power, Mâra caused a hundred and a thousand clouds to arise, and spread in the ten directions the noise of a thunder-storm; a hundred lightnings played, rain-drops fell, in size like a palm tree, ploughing the earth, and bearing along many trees; but when it approached Siddhârtha, it did not wet even the hem of his robe; it was refreshing to him, as it fell like a shower of water lilies, did him honour, and went away. Mâra again looked to see whether he had given up the desire to become Buddha, or to see into what ocean he had been driven by the force of the stream; but when he saw the renowned mouth of the prince, shining like a full moon, he became angry as a goaded elephant, and he thought, 'I will now destroy him by crushing him to pieces,' intending to bring upon him a shower of rocks. He therefore hurled through the sky a hundred thousand burning mountains, twenty or thirty miles in size; but when they approached the prince, by the power of his obedience to the precepts, they were converted into garlands of sweet flowers, and arranged themselves in order around him, like a floral offering."

Then follow showers of weapons, burning charcoal, fiery ashes, burning sand, hot filth, and four-fold darkness,—all with like effect:—

"Thus these nine dangers, wind, rain, rocks, weapons, charcoal, ashes, sand, mud, and darkness did no harm whatever to Siddhârtha, but were converted into offerings. When Mâra perceived this as he was unable to approach the prince, he said angrily to his army from a distance, 'All of you, seize Siddhârtha, pierce him, cut him, break him to peices, grind him to powder, destroy his desire to become Buddha, do not let him escape.' Saying this, he mounted his elephant *Girimêkhala;* and brandishing his formidable discus on every side, he approached the prince, and threw it towards him. Were this weapon to be thrown against Mahâ-Mêru, it would cleave the mountain in twain as if it were a bambu; were it cast into the ocean, its waters would be dried up; were it hurled into the sky, it would prevent the falling of rain for twelve years; but though it has such mighty energy it could not be brought to approach the prince who was seeking the Buddhaship; through his great merit it rose and fell in the air like a dry leaf, and afterwards remained in splendour above his head like a canopy of flowers. The warriors of Mâra meanwhile said to each other, 'It is to no purpose now to look for Siddhârtha, as he is undoubtedly destroyed; never before this time did our divine master throw the discus; to look for him now would be useless;' yet after posing for a time a hundred thousand rocks, they hurled them in the same direction, which, however, became only like an offering of sweet-scented flowers. The *dêvas* who had remained hid among the *sakwala* rocks now lifted up their heads to see what was going on; and exclaimed in fear, 'This day the glory of Siddhârtha disappears; Mâra has thrown the discus!' But when Mâra saw that he could not shake the prince by the power of this formidable weapon, he went in front of him, burning with anger like the fire at the end of a *kalpa*, and rolling round his red eyes he took his thousand weapons into his thousand hands, and brandishing them before the prince he said, 'I will take thee by thy two legs, and hurl thee into the next *sakwala*; begone from my throne.'

When former Bodhisattvas received the Buddhaship, the Mâras who came to oppose them saw at once the glory of their sacred mouth (which extended to the *sakwala-gala*), trembled, and were overcome. But upon the present occasion, Mâra had an advantage not possessed by his predecessors in the same struggle.

For this there was a cause. In the *Wessantara* birth Bodhisattva gave away his children, Jali and Krishnajinâ, to the Brahman Jujaka, who beat them until they bled, and in other ways used them cruelly. On account of these hardships, Krishnajinâ looked up submissively in her father's face, weeping; at which he felt exceedingly sorrowful, from the strength of his parental affection, and began to consider whether he should not by force take his children again. It was on account of this hesitancy that Mâra now received power to approach the Bô-tree, and say with a tremendous voice 'Begone from my throne'! Notwithstanding this stern command, the prince had no fear; he answered with a smile, speaking in a sweet voice from his lotos-like mouth, 'Sinful Mâra! to gain this throne I have practised the *pâramitâs* during four *asankyas* and a *kaplaksha.* I am therefore the rightful owner of this throne. How canst thou possess it, who hast never accomplished a single

the Bodhi tree, with his right hand pointing to the earth (*Bhumisparśa mudrâ*) and the left in his lap, while the drum of the *dêvas* is being beat above.

The painting has now nearly all disappeared, though there are still some fragments on the roof of Buddhas painted of a yellow colour.

---

pâramitâ?' When he said this, Mâra became still more enraged, like a fire into which oil is poured, and replied, 'I have given more in alms than thou hast given; I have accomplished more *pâramitâs*.' The prince asked, 'Where are your witnesses?' On which Mâra stretched out his thousand arms towards his attendant army, and said, 'Here are my witnesses!' Then the warriors replied, 'We are witnesses!' Lifting up their hands at the same time; and the sound was enough to cleave the earth; it was like the roar of the sea, and struck the *Brahma-loka*. Mâra proceeded, 'Oh, prince Siddhârtha; so great an army has become witness that I have accomplished the *pâramitâs*; that you have fulfilled them, produce a single witness.' 'Your witnesses,' replied the prince, 'are alive and partial; mine are not alive, and they are without any partiality;' and like lightning launched from a red cloud he stretched forth his hand from his robe. He said further, 'When it was announced by Dipankara Buddha that in due time I should become a Buddha, and I was reflecting on the accomplishment of the thirty *pâramitâs*, the ten thousand *sakwalas* cried aloud; and thou thyself didst say, Sâdhu! Leaving out the other births in the *Wessantara* birth, when I was eighty years of age and determined to offer an alms; when I was eight years of age and determined to offer an alms; when I gave the elephants, and 700 of all the articles that I possessed, and went from the city to the rock of Wankagiri, and I gave my children, and my queen Mandri-dêvî, and the shower of water lilies fell; at these seven periods thou thyself didst cry out (in approbation), 'Why did not the earth cry out at the utterance of thy lying witnesses?' At the same time he streched out his hand towards the earth; and the earth gave out a hundred and a thousand sounds at the same instant, like the striking of a drum the size of a *sakwala* with a stick the size of Mahâ-Méru. Then the earth opened, and mountains of fire rose up from the 136 hells, and the army of Mâra fled away with a great noise, like leaves driven by the wind, each in a different direction. They threw down their ornaments and weapons, and their outer garments; and covering their faces with both hands, without looking at their leader, they went off in great trepidation. The elephant, *Girimêkhala*, fell upon his knees, trembled with fear, threw down Mâra from his back, curled up his trunk and thrust the end into his mouth, put his tail between his legs, growled fiercely, and without looking at his master, fled away. When the *Déva* fell to the ground, bereft of his thousand weapons, he exclaimed, 'Oh, prince Siddhârtha, I perceive that thou art powerful, and that thou art glorious; thou hast fulfilled the thirty *pâramitâs*; I will proclaim thy courage to the world; I will proclaim thy power; forgive, forgive!' Three times did he make this exclamation, after which he fled to his own world; but being ashamed to look at his attendants he lay down and concealed his face.

The *dêvas* of this *sakwala* now called out to the *dêvas* of the next, 'Mâra is overcome, and has fled; our prince Siddhârtha is conqueror! The *Nâgas* of this *sakwala* called out to those in the next; as well as the *Garundas*, and *Brahmas*. The *S'akras* of the 10,000 *sakwalas*, the *Mahâ-Brahmas*, *Nâgas*, *Garundas*, *Suparnnas*, and other beings brought celestial flowers and perfumes; assembling around the prince, they put their hands to their foreheads and made obeisance.

As Mâra was unable to bear the ridicule that the *dêvas* heaped upon him on account of his discomfiture, he arose from his couch, and came to a certain place in Jambudwîpa, where he assumed the appearance of a traveller; but his mind was still filled with sorrow, as he reflected that notwithstanding all his opposition, the prince had become a Buddha, and would in a little time preach the *bana*, by which many things would obtain *nirvâna*. Whilst indulging these reflections he made ten marks upon the ground, as there were ten things that were presented to his mind and as he tried to reckon up the many hundreds of thousands of ways in which he was inferior to Buddha, the marks were extended to twelve.

When Tanhâ, Ratî, and Rangâ, the daughters of Mâra, perceived that their father had vanished from the *dêva-loka*, they looked with their divine eyes to see whither he had gone; and when they had discovered the place of his retreat, they went to him in the snapping of a finger, and enquired why he was so disconsolate. Having learnt the cause, they told him to become cheerful, as they themselves would overcome the prince; and when Mâra replied that their attempts would be in vain, they said that there was no being whatever who could withstand their wiles even for a single moment; they then transformed themselves into 600 beautiful maidens of different ages, their dress being arranged in the most wanton manner. Approaching the prince, they praised the beauty of his person, and asked why he remained under the tree; had he no queen, or had he quarrelled with her, or was it to meet some one whom he loved that he had come to this spot? But Siddhârtha remained unmoved. Tanhâ continued to praise his beauty, and to flatter him; and when this was to no purpose, she reminded him that at other times he had sought the enjoyment of what he now refused. But Buddha did not even look at the tempters, and after they had long tried to overcome him without effect, they fled away."—S. Hardy, *Manual of Budhism*.

CAVE XXVII.

Cave XXVII is the last accessible Vihâra. The front is broken away, and a huge fragment of rock lies before the cave, which is about 43½ feet wide and 31 deep, without pillars. It has never been finished, and the ante-chamber to the shrine is only blocked out. There are three cells in the left side, two in the back, and one in the portion of the left side that remains.

CAVES XXVIII and XXIX.

Cave XXVIII is the beginning of a Chaitya-cave, high upon the scarp between Nos. XXI and XXII; but little more than the top of the great arch of the window has been completed.

Cave XXIX is the verandah of a Vihâra beyond XXVII, supported by six rough-hewn pillars and two pilasters. No. XXVIII is very difficult of access and XXIX is inaccessible.

NOTE.

KHOSRU II. (PARWIS) AND PULAKÊSI II.

After the above was in type I received from Mr. J. Fergusson a proof of a paper lately read by him before the Royal Asiatic Society, *On the Identification of the Portrait of Chosroes II. among the Paintings in the Caves at Ajaṇṭâ*,—which is so interesting historically, in relation to the age of some of the paintings in Cave I (No. 17, pp. 22 and 26), that I give the following long extract from it :—

" If we may assume, " he says," for the present at least, that the person represented in these pictures is a Persian king, there are other reasons besides his date which would lead us to identify him with Chosroes (A.D. 591—628).[1] There is a class of late Sassanian coins, not unfrequently found in India, which have engraved on the face of them in good Indian Devanagari characters the name of Vasu Dêva. These coins all numismatists agree in assigning to Khosru II.,[2] and the fact of his using Indian characters on his coins shows that he—and he only apparently of Sassanian kings—had some intimate connexion with that country.[3] Taking all these facts together, I cannot but think that we are justified in assuming that the principal figure in these four pictures is meant to represent the great Chosroes ; and if this be so there can be no manner of doubt but that the woman by his side is the fair Shirîn, so celebrated in eastern story for her beauty and adventures. She is the only woman, so far as I know, who appears in any of the bas-reliefs of the Sassanian kings in any part of Persia. She occurs, however, at Naksh-i-Rustam with the king and a third person, who may or may not be Ferhad.[4] At Takht-i-Bostan the same triad appear, but in greater state,[5] and this time without the least doubt who is intended to be represented. Curiously enough, in this last bas-relief Shirîn holds a vessel in her left hand, by no means unlike that held by one of the maidens in the picture. In her right hand she holds a ring with the Sassanian fillet. Her face, with that of all the principal personages in these bas-reliefs, has been too much damaged by the Mohammedans for the features to be made out, and, even if uninjured, it is extremely unlikely that we should be able to recognize in paintings by a foreign hand the features as portrayed by a native sculptor in a state representation of the Queen. At the same time it is necessary to point out that though all the four paintings at Ajaṇṭâ are certainly intended to represent the same persons, they can hardly be recognized by their likenesses. The best and finest is certainly (Mr. Griffiths's) No. 4, which we probably may assume to be the nearest approach to the Persian original they had to copy. No. 20 is certainly by an inferior artist, and No. 64 is still further removed from the perfection of the first. In it Shirîn's face and neck are represented as black, not the black of the complexions of other figures in pictures in the same cave, but a cold grey black, as if the artist had been using a dark ground or had employed some preparation of lead which had turned black. The features and dress are the same as on the other pictures, but it evidently had been entrusted to an inferior artist, to copy from the original design.

" In like manner, it is equally impossible to identify the portrait of the King in these pictures from any of the sculptured representations of him—there are no pictures—found in Persia. At Takht-i-Bostan, where there is no doubt as to the person represented, the countenance of the King has been so completely defaced as to render recognition impossible ; but in one of the hunting-scenes, that on the right hand in the niche, the features are not so completely obliterated, and though the nose is gone, the burly form of the face, the short

---

[1] I have been informed that in the Salle d' Apollon in the Louvre at Paris, there is an onyx cup, on which is engraved the portrait of a king, acknowledged to be that of Chosroes II., seated in the same attitude, and holding a cup in the right hand, as represented in this picture. I have not myself seen the cup, and have been unable to procure or gain access to any engraving of it ; and am consequently unable to say how far it can be quoted as confirming the views expressed in this paper.

[2] *Ariana Antiqua*, p. 400, pl. xvii ; Thomas's Prinsep, vol. i., p. 402 *et seq.* ; vol. ii., p. 114.

[3] When I was writing my *History of Indian Architecture*, I saw Mr. Griffiths's paintings at South Kensington : but, as there were then no labels upon them, I assumed, erroneously, that they were copied from the roof of Cave No. XVII, which is considerably earlier than No. I, and consequently jumped to the conclusion—in a note, p. 157—that the king must be Bahram Gaur, whose visit to India and marriage with an Indian Princess is celebrated in Indian and Persian romances.

[4] Texier, *Armenie et la Perse*, vol. ii., pl. 133 ; Ker Porter, vol. i., pl. 19.

[5] Flandin et Coste, *Perse Ancienne*, vol. i., p. 9 ; Ker Porter, vol. ii., pl. 62.

beard, and the general contour of the whole,[1] so similar to what is represented at Ajaṇṭâ, that it may almost be assumed to be the same person. Even the head-dress[2] is similar though somewhat lower on the crown; though all this is now unfortunately so indistinct that if there were no other evidence it would be difficult to base any argument upon it."

"I had proceeded thus far in my investigations when Dr. G. Bühler happened to call. I showed him what I had done, and explained to him that the only remaining difficulty was to ascertain the name of the King, represented in the great fresco on the walls of this cave, who was receiving the Persian deputation. From Hiouen Thsang's description of India at that age, it appeared to me there were only three kings who were at all likely to be so portrayed. Either it must be Śîlâditya of Kanauj, or Dhruvasena or Batta of Valabhi, or Pulakêśi, King of Mahârashṭra. He immediately said it must be the latter. His friend Professor Nöldeke, of Strasburg, in translating Tabari from the Arabic, has found the name of that king in conjunction with that of Chosroes, so as to render it nearly certain that he is the king indicated, and he at once promised to procure me a translation of the paragraph in question. In due time I received a communication from him, which seems to me to leave no room for hesitation.

"When after his defeat in the battle at Nineveh the unfortunate king was dethroned and thrown into prison, his son Shiruyieh sought for some excuse for putting him to death, in order to succeed to the throne. For this purpose he drew up an indictment in eleven counts, detailing certain crimes of which he accused his father. The second of these, in the words of the Persian recension of Tabari, was 'That he had imprisoned the grandchildren of his father in order to prevent them creating a posterity, and had denied to them what God had permitted to man,'[3] alluding to the birth of Yezdegird as related in a previous passage (page 329). In answer to this the dethroned king pleads, 'that he did so because the astrologers had announced that, during the reign of a grandson of his, the kingdom of Persia would be destroyed, and that in casting his (Shiruyieh's) horoscope it was predicted that he himself should perish by the hand of his own eldest son, and he would consequently have been justified in putting him to death, but spared him from parental affection.' He then adds, in the Arabic version, 'Two years ago, Pulakêśi, King of India, sent to us, in the thirty-sixth year of our reign, ambassadors carrying a letter imparting to us various news, and presents for us, for you, and our other sons. He also wrote a letter to each of you. To you he presented—don't you remember it?—an elephant, a sword, a white falcon and a piece of gold brocade. When we looked at the presents and at the letters, we remarked that yours bore the mark 'Private' on the cover in the Indian language. Then we ordered that the presents and other letters should be delivered to each of you, but we kept back your letter, on account of the remark written on the outside. We then sent for an Indian scribe, had the seal broken, and the letter read. The contents were :—'Rejoice and be of good cheer, for on the day Dai ba Âdbar, of the thirty-eighth year of the reign of Chosroes, thou wilt be crowned king and become ruler of the whole empire. Signed, Pulakêśi.' But we closed this letter with our seal, and gave it into the keeping of our consort Shirîn."

"The thirty-sixth year of the reign of Chosroes corresponds with 18 June 625, to 17 June 626. Chosroes was dethroned on the 25th February 628 (Dai be Adhar), and put to death a few days later. 'The story of the defence,' the Professor goes on to remark, 'made by Chosroes at his trial can hardly be considered as historical; but the fact that he received an embassy from an Indian king in 625 need not be doubted on that account. Tabari in this part of his narrative followed a Pehlvi work written shortly after the King's death, but before the Arabian conquest, as is evident from the style in which it is written, and from the in-

---

[1] Ker Porter, vol. ii., pl 64. Whenever they represent the same person or thing, his delineations are to be perferred to either those of Texier or of Flandin and Coste.

[2] In the bas-reliefs at Shapur, representing the defeat of Valerian, the King Shapur holds his son Hormuzd by the right hand, and he is represented with a head-dress nearly similar to that worn by the King in this picture. Unfortunately Flandin and Coste (*Voyage en Perse,* vol. i., pl 49) mistake him for a Roman captive and put manacles on his feet, but both Texier (vol. ii., pl. 146) and Ker Porter represent him without these adornments, and with the crimped streamers of the Sassanians.

[3] Tabari, translated by Zotenberg, vol. ii., p. 334. All the incidents accompanying the dethronement and death of Khosru II. will be found narrated in Zotenberg's translation from the Persian recension of Tabari, vol. ii, p. 328 *et seq.*, though in less detail than in the Arabic version, and without the king's name.

timate acquaintance the author shows in all that concerns the King's affairs, in which he was evidently deeply interested.'[1]

"Of course, it is not contended that the letter which the messengers are presenting to the King in the fresco on the wall, is the identical letter alluded to by Chosroes.[2] Quite the contrary. The letter there represented is *from* the Persian *to* the Indian king, but taken together with the circumstances above narrated, may be considered sufficient to establish the fact that an active correspondence did take place at this time between the two kings and that there is at least no improbability that the King on the throne is Pulakêśi, and that the messengers really came from the unfortunate King Khosru the Second.

"That the messengers are Persians is nearly certain from their complexion and general appearance as well as from their costume, which is carefully contrasted with those of the Indians in the same picture. Whoever they were, they certainly are a people who inhabited the countries west of the Indus and south of the Hindu Kush, and who reached their destination on horseback, for their horses are shown in the picture.

"The most distinguishing feature in the costume of these messengers is the high conical caps they all wear. It is not, however, necessary to go back to the sculptures of Nineveh for examples of this form of head-dress, as Babu Rajandra proposes, as such are still worn by the Kurds, and other tribes in the north of Persia, at the present day.[3] In fact, their whole appearance and dress are such as leave almost no doubt of their nationality, and so far confirm the inferences to be drawn from the narrative of Tabari.

"Before going further it may be as well to remark that there are few dates in mediæval history so well established from inscription as the accession of Pulakêśi to the throne in 609-10,[4] and no fact more certain than that he was in the full plenitude of his power when Hiouen Thsang visited his court in 639-40. He certainly was, if not the most powerful, at least the second King of India during the last years of Chosroes' reign. His successful wars with Harshavardhana or Śîlâditya of Kanauj, then the paramount power in India, having placed him in exactly the same position that same Marâṭhas attained to just 1000 years later by the successful wars which Śivaji and his successors waged against Aurangzeb and the Emperors of Delhi. Nothing is more likely than that Pulakêśi should have cherished a Persian alliance during a struggle for existance with his sovereign, who aspired to be Lord of the Five Indias.

"It may also be observed, as confirmatory of the above, that Ajaṇṭâ was situated within the limits of the kingdom of Pulakêśi ; for, after visiting him at his capital—whether this was at Kalyâṇ, or more probably Bâdâmi—Hiouen Thsang remarks :—'Sur les frontiéres orientales du royaume, il y a une grande montagne'—'Anciennement il y avait un couvent qui avait été construit dans une sombre vallée, ses batimens elevés a ses salles profondes occupaient les larges ouvertures des rochers, et s'appuyaient sur les pics. Ses pavillons et ses tours a double étage étaient adossés aux cavernes et regardaient la vallée.'[5] It would be difficult to find words to describe more correctly the form and position of the caves at Ajaṇṭâ, and there only, for no other series is so distinctly in a valley. Generally the caves are situated on the faces of the hills, and visible on all sides. At Ajaṇṭa alone they are buried in a deep and secluded valley piercing the table-land.

"Unfortunately we are unable to judge of the personal appearance of Pulakêśi, as a more ruthless destroyer than the Moslem bigot has entirely removed from the wall the plas-

---

[1] The name of the King in the codex is ورمسا. By another author, Dinawari, it is written ورمسسا and with the diacritical points قرميسا QRMISA. The diacritical points, however, when used in writing foreign names, have no authority. We may, therefore, assume فرميشا PhRMIShA is intended, or, as the Arabs use *Ph* for the Persian *P* and *I* for the Persian *Ê* we must write his name PRMÊShA. At the same time as *R* and *L* are written with the same sign in Pehlvi, so is *R* to be taken as a false mode of expressing *L*. As *M* may be substituted for *K* (*Q*) in the Arabic, or in the Pehlvi, it follows that the name may be correctly represented in Pehlvi by PLKSA and read as Pulikêsa (Nöldeke).

[2] I am by no means sure that it is a *letter* which is intended in the painting.—J. B.

[3] Malcolm, *History of Persia*, vol. ii., p. 602.

[4] Burgess, vol. iii. of *Archæological Reports* of Western India, p. 132. Inscription translated by J. F. Fleet, Bo.C.S.

[5] *Memoires des Contrées Occidentales*, vol. ii., p. 151.

ter on which his countenance was depicted, and it cannot now be recovered.[1] But the general effect of the painted architecture of his palace, and the appearance of his court, still remain portrayed with a truthfulness that leaves little to be desired. In the centre of the picture the King is represented seated on a throne (*chârpai*), his elbows resting on a cushion, under a canopy, of very graceful form. In front of him, seated on the ground, is the graceful form of a woman bearing a *chaurî*, and right and left of the King are two other females, with similar symbols of royalty, and behind them two gigantic dwarpals or porters. On his right hand, on the ground, are two females, one of whom, at least, is playing on some musical instrument; and on his left hand, also on the ground, are four figures in front of the throne, two females and two men. The first of these, nearest the King, bears in his hands a tray, containing what I take to be the return presents and curiously enough among these is a little golden image of an elephant, which may be as likely a present for Pulakêśi to send to Shiruyieh as a living specimen of that animal. But against this theory it may be remarked that the white falcon mentioned in the text was certainly a living specimen of its class, and from the sculptures at Takht-i-Bostan we know that Chosroes had many elephants which he employed in hunting. All, therefore, that can be said is, that if there is any foundation for this theory, it is that the painter may have found it more convenient to introduce a golden counterfeit rather than a full-sized animal into the picture. The fair-complexioned figure standing up to the left of the throne may be the prime minister or vizier, but from the staff in his hand (gold stick), he more probably is only the master of the ceremonies. The other figures do not seem to have any special function, but altogether they make up a very graphic representation of what we can fancy an Indian Court to have been at the beginning of the seventh century of our era.

"I do not know how all this may strike others, but to me it seems to make out a very strong case for believing that the portraits on the roof of Cave No. I at Ajaṇṭâ are really those of Khosru II., surnamed Parwis, the Chosroes of the Greeks, and of his wife, the fair and celebrated Shirîn; and further, that the great fresco on the wall represents Pulakêśi, King of Mahârâshṭra, receiving an embassy from the Persian King, and dimissing it with the customary complimentary presents.

"If this is so, I need hardly add that it is by far the most satisfactory synchronism we have yet got out of these paintings, as it proves the date of the transaction represented on the walls, as one that took place 625–6, though the painting may be somewhat later, but would hardly have been painted after the death of the king in 628 A.D.

"It is almost equally satisfactory—if it can be established—to have contemporary portraits of two such celebrated persons, as the king who took Jerusalem and carried off the Holy Cross to Persia,[2] and of his wife, regarding whom, as Sir John Malcom says, '1,000 volumes have been written in her praise,' and she was certainly the most celebrated female in Eastern history since the time of Cleopatra and Zenobia, and, as far as the East is concerned, more celebrated than either of these great Queens."

---

[1] When Dr. Bird visited Ajantâ, he is said to have cut out some twenty or thirty of the most interesting faces from these frescoes, with the intention of presenting them to the Museum at Bombay. But, as might be expected, they were so carelessly packed, that all except one or two were reduced to powder before reaching their destination. Whether this was one of these, or whether it was destroyed by some other British barbarian, cannot now be ascertained.

[2] It is rather a curious coincidence that six years ago I should have been asked by Dr. Tristram to restore the design of the façade of a palace of this same king, some fragments of which he had found to the eastward of the Dead Sea, during a journey which resulted in the publication of his book entitled *The Land of Moab* (Murray, 1873). To it the reader is referred for some further particulars regarding Ferhad and Shirin, though full details are only to be found in works especially devoted to Persian history.

PAINTINGS IN BAGH CAVE-TEMPLES.

The Caves of Bâgh, in the district of Râth in the south of Malwa, are less known than those of Ajaṇṭâ; and having been excavated in a soft sandstone, they are much ruined, several of them having fallen in altogether. Like those of Ajaṇṭâ they have been painted, and but for its occupation by Yogis, the only one that is fairly entire might have had its wall and ceiling paintings almost complete to the present day. They have been entirely covered with soot, however, and so are quite lost.

The third and fourth caves to the right are both very large, the first being a large square hall, and the other a long room with two rows of pillars from end to end of it. These two caves have had a single verandah about 220 feet in length, and it is on the back wall of this that the only considerable fragments are now left, exposed to all the vicissitudes of the weather.

In this long verandah beginning at the left side of the left door (or window ?) of the smaller cave, where the first fragments are distinct, and going to the left, we have—

I. Two men clothed to the neck,—*bhikshus*—seated among plantain trees with flower trays in their laps, talking. In front are trees and creepers, and below a *lotâ* with a cup inverted in the mouth of it; and beside it is what seems to be a stand, with clothes hung on it, and, at the foot, two water vessels, one on the other; to the left is a flagon and another *ghara*.

II. To the left again is the Aśoka tree; and then a palm with a creeper twisting round it. Facing this, are two red elephants and a white one with riders, and below the first is a man seated with some instrument in his hand and a blue scarf. In front of him is a man with a blue Nepalese sword, and below, or in the foreground of the white elephant, is a horse saddled with a man on the other side of it. Behind the white elephant is another with the points of the tusks painted blue and ridden by a man with an *ankuśa* with the side prong reverted; and behind him is a man in blue striped cloth, seated near the rump of the elephant. Below this is a large conventional gateway, from which the *sowâri* proceeds to the left. On the upper elephant is the driver and three women. The first and third clothed to their necks, the middle one with a necklace and a drum under her arm. On the lower elephant all three women have jewelled necklaces, and the middle one is the more clothed, and looks back to the third. This elephant is met by a man on a green horse.

In front of the upper elephant is a man with a long spear, and before him is another large elephant, and then the head of a white one advancing with his face turned nearly towards the spectator,—he is ridden by a man. Below is a man on horseback, and then a great man on an elephant with his *chattri* bearer behind him. His hair is done up in Persian fashion, in locks all round, looking in front like a modern school-girl and with a ball of his hair tied behind in a cloth like a chignon. He has no jewels. Beyond him is the conventional hill, behind which part of the procession seems to advance. From behind it, a man in blue clothing comes on a white horse, and in the foreground is another on a red horse, his hair in curls. In front of these are four more riders—one in blue, and below, another with his hair in curls. Then above to the left is a figure (man or woman uncertain) with flowers in the back hair and the umbrella borne over his (or her) head—wearing a white dress spotted with blue, and coming close

WALL ELEVATIONS OF CAVE I.

Page 9.

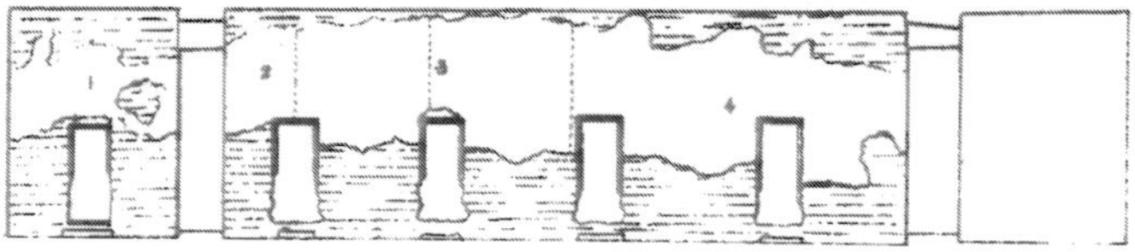

1 *Left side wall.*

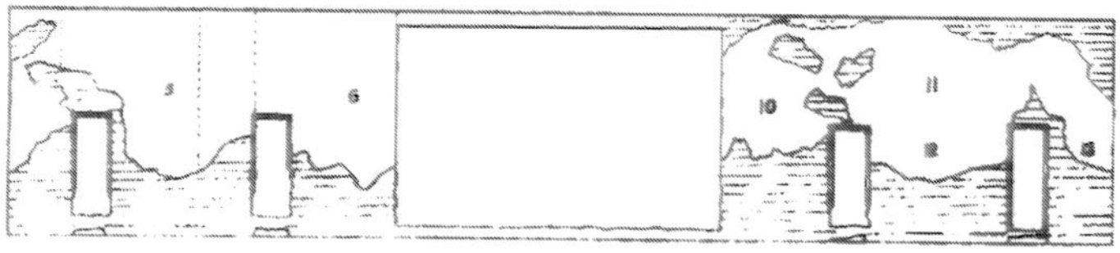

2 *Back wall.*

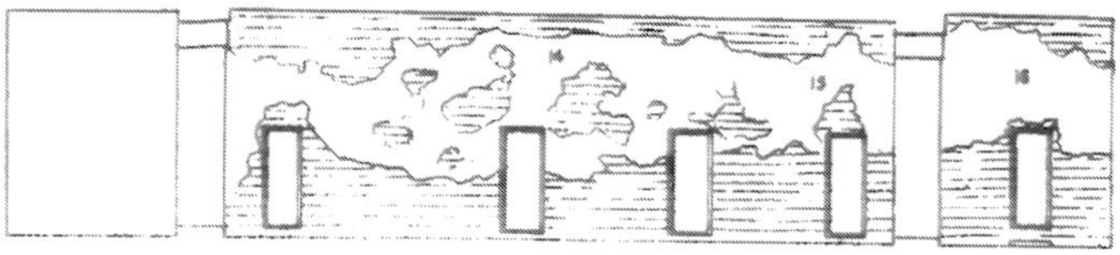

3 *Right side wall.*

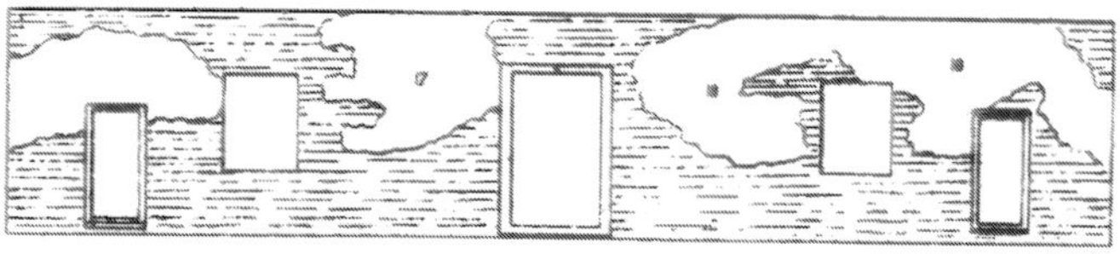

4 *Front wall, inside.*

Scale of … *feet.*

Govt. Photozincographic Office, Poona, 1879.

H. Cousens delt.

Plate II.

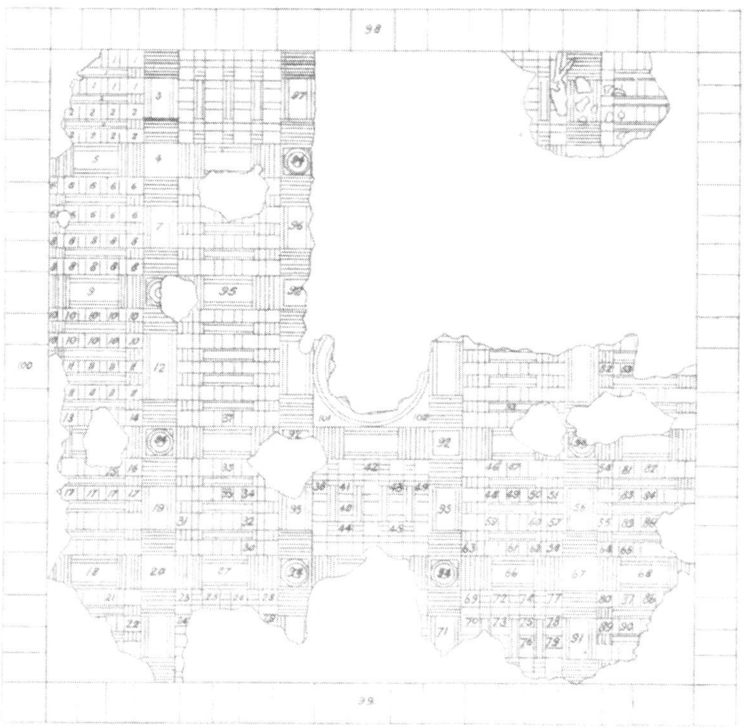

Front side.

Scale of 10 0 10 20 30 feet.

CEILING OF CAVE I.

page. 25.

Gov^t Photozincographic Office, Poona, 1879.

WALL PAINTING IN CAVE I - PART OF Nº 12

page 10.

Govt Photozincographic Office Poona 1879

Jayrao Raghoba
H. Cousens } delt.

Plate IV.

1 FRIEZE OVER LEFT CHAPEL OF CAVE I.

page 6.

2 GROUP OF IRANIANS FROM CEILING OF CAVE I.

page 26.

Govt. Photozincographic Office, Poona, 1879

Plate V.

CAVE II

page 28.

Elevation of left wall

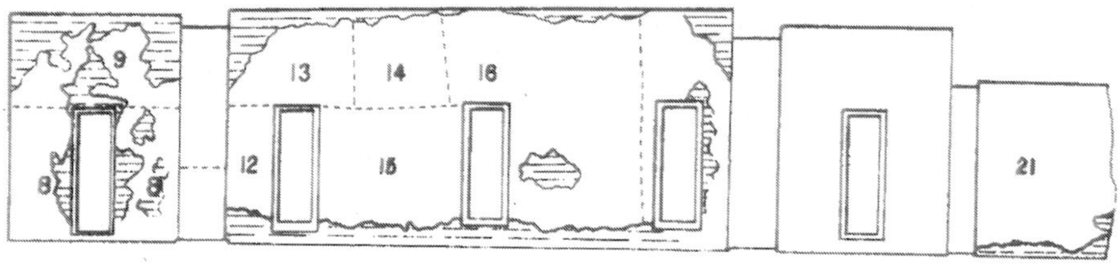

1

Elevation of back wall

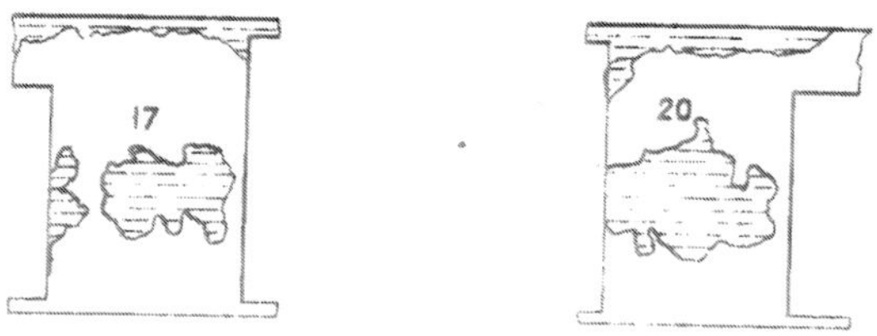

2

Elevation of right wall

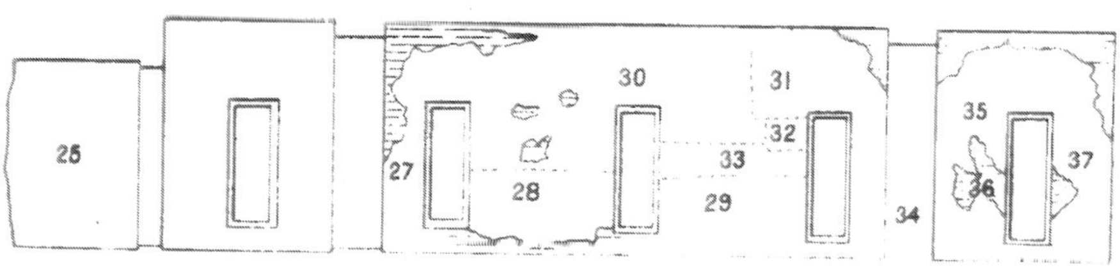

3

Scale of 10 0 10 20 30 40 50 feet

Govt Photozincographic Office Poona 1879

H Cousens delt.

SCULPTURE IN ONE OF THE BACK CHAPELS OF CAVE II.

Page 28

Burgess

Gov. Photozincographic Office, Poona 1879

Jayrao Raghoba delt.

Plate VII.

1 BOAT FROM WALL PAINTINGS IN CAVE II.
page 38

2 CHADANTA ELEPHANT FROM CAVE X
page 50

Plate VIII.

FIGURES FROM THE OLDEST PAINTING IN CAVE X.

page. 57.

Jayrau Raghoba delt. Photozincographed Govt. Office Poona 1879 J. Burgess

Plate IX.

FIGURES FROM THE OLDEST PAINTING IN CAVE X.

page 57.

Jayrao Raghoba delt. Photozincographed Govt. Office Poona, 1879 J. Burgess

Plate X.

GROUP FROM THE OLDEST PAINTING IN CAVE X

Plate XI.

9

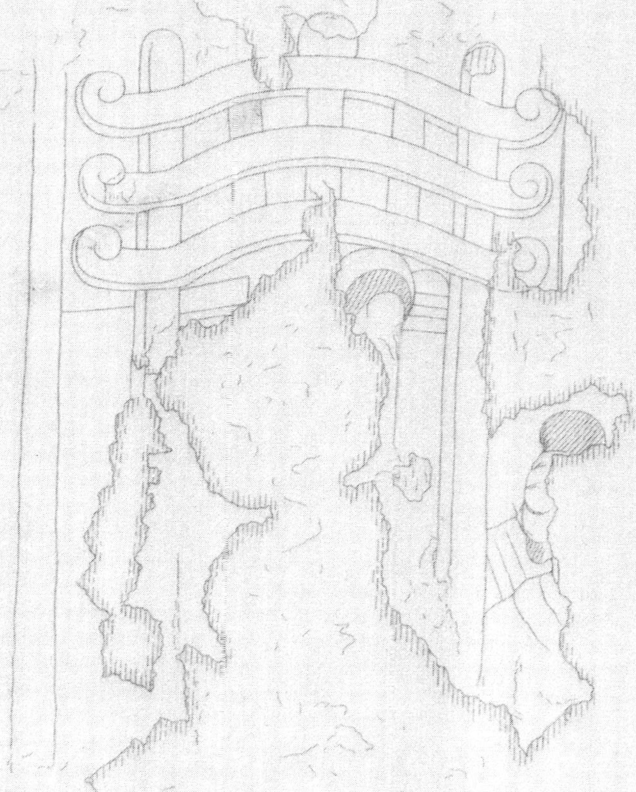

10

TWO GATEWAYS FROM THE WALL PAINTINGS IN CAVE X.

J. Burgess

Jayrao Raghoba delt.

Plate XII.

WALL ELEVATIONS IN CAVE XVI.

page 57.

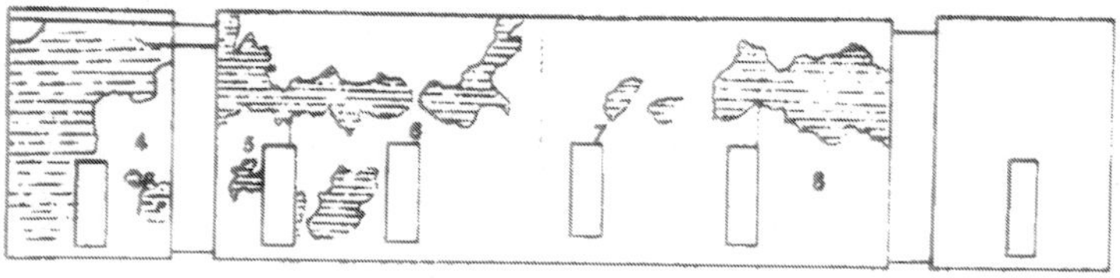

1 Left side wall.

2 Back wall.

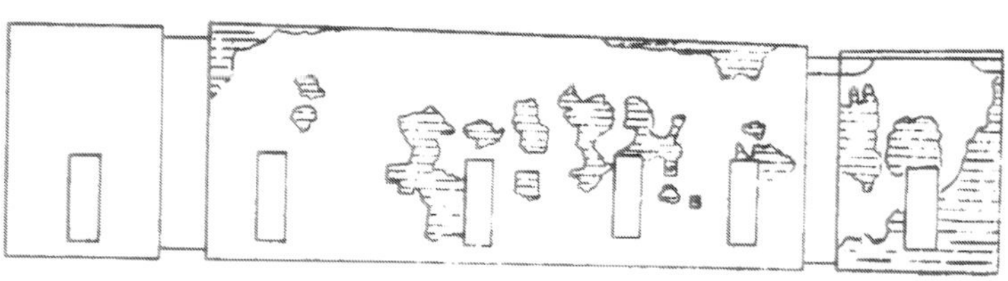

3 Right side wall.

Scale of 10 0 10 20 30 40 50 60 feet.

Govt Photozincographic Office, Poona 1879

H Cousens delt

1 NÂGA RÂJA
page 57.

2 BUDDHA TEACHING, FROM CAVE XVI
page 56. VI

S. J. Pacheco delt.

Govt. Photozincographic Office Poona 1879

Plate XIV.

3. BUDDHA AND A RÂJA, FROM CAVE XVI
page 59. VI

4. LION FROM A SINHÂSANA PAINTED IN CAVE XVI
page 59 VIII

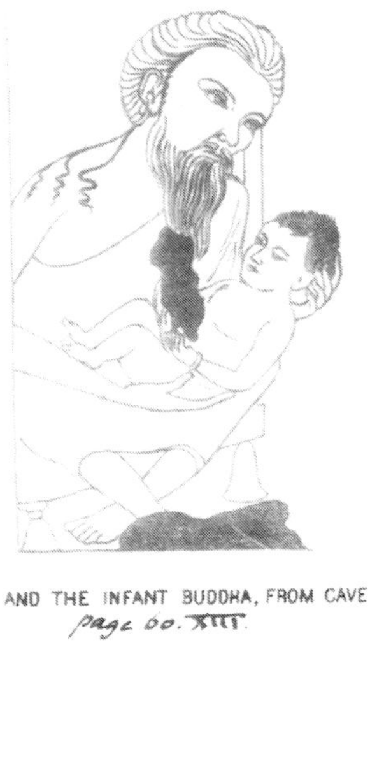

5. ASITA AND THE INFANT BUDDHA, FROM CAVE XVI
page 60. XIII

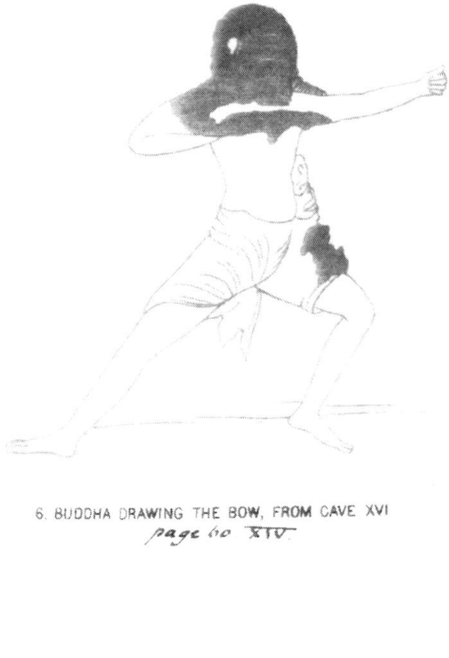

6. BUDDHA DRAWING THE BOW, FROM CAVE XVI
page 60 XIV

Plate XV.

WALL ELEVATIONS OF CAVE XVII.

page 61.

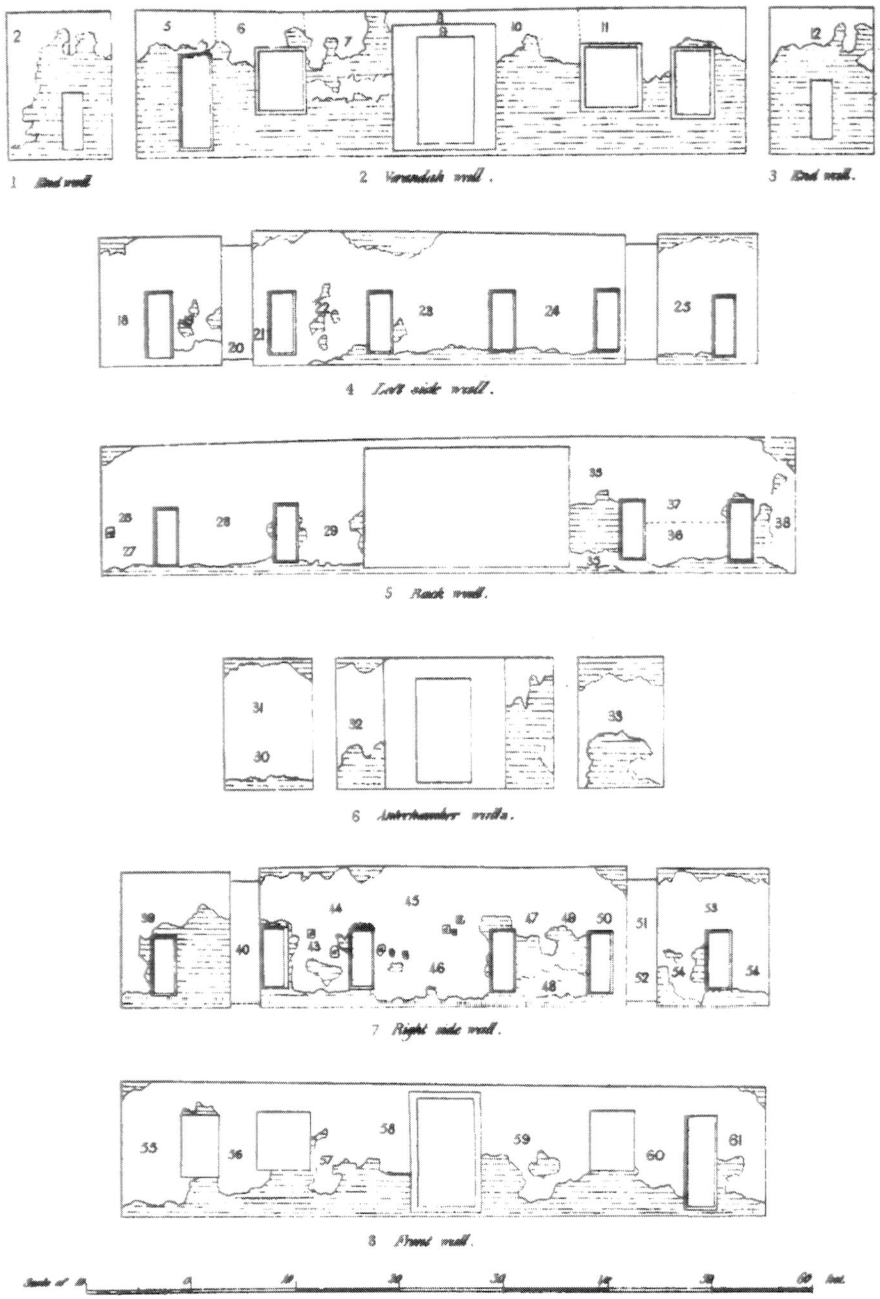

Govt Photozincographic Office, Poona. 1879

H Cousens delt

Plate XVI.

PORTION OF PAINTING FROM THE END OF THE VERANDA IN CAVE XVII.

page 62

Govt. Photozincographic Office, Poona. 1879

H. Cousens delt.

Plate XVII.

1. YAKSHAS FROM CAVE XVII

2. BUDDHA AND THE ELEPHANT FROM CAVE XVII

page 64

Plate XVIII.

3 WALL SCENE FROM CAVE XVII

page 68

Govt Photozincographic Office, Poona, 1879

Plate XIX.

4 LANDING AND CORONATION OF VIJAYA
IN CEYLON FROM CAVE XVII

Govt. Photozincographic Office Poona 1879

BUDDHA TRIED BY MÂRA

page 85.

J. Burgess

Redrawn and photozincographed
Govt. Office Poona 1879

Jayrao Raghoba delt.

Inscriptions from Cave XXVI at Ajantā

Inscription from Cave XXVI at Ajantâ

page 83.

Photozincographed Govt. Office, Poona, 1879

Inscription from Cave XXVI at Ajantá

page 83.

round the neck. To the left are at least four more men on horseback, a figure with a blue bow, and another man.

III. Here a painted wall divides from the next scene in which most of the figures are females.

First is a group of seven figures—one a man fully clothed, with long curls, perhaps singing—stands in the middle, and the six women are round him. Two women play cymbals; one more bejewelled than the rest, is half nude, and has her hair in short small ringlets, and she and two others have each a pair of short sticks (*bones* ?) which they are beating together. Another half nude female has a drum slung over her shoulder by a cord, while she looks round with a roguish leer.

IV. The next group has six women round a man with a spotted coat, a blue and grey cap on his head, large earrings, and a great pointed collar and necklace; and to the right below are two *mridangas*. Three women have small cymbals, the other three short sticks (or *bones*), and the seventh a drum. They seem greatly interested. This sort of amusement is called *hallisaka*.

V. To the left are six men, like *arhats* or *bhikshus* sitting in the clouds, and below part of another *hallisaka* group—the heads only of seven persons being left.

VI. Over the door of the *Rang mahâl* or painted cave, as it is called, sit two râja-like people—one with a square crown, the other with a pointed one, and before them, to the right, two men with necklaces, and all on cushions. Beside the second râja sits a small blue child. A wall then divides from an interior in which sit two women, one in the undress and jewels of a rânî, with her hand against her cheek as if sad. The *dâsî* beside her holds part of her dress to her face as if crying—the left she has placed on the rânî's breast.

VII. To the left are fragments of figures, too much destroyed to make anything of them.

All is gone from this, over the window to the next door.

VIII. Between it and the left window has been a large crowned figure with a nimbus, and *gandharvas*, but all is much destroyed. Over the window is a nude female seated and some other figures with plants.

IX. Between the window and left end door is a large piece of painting, in which are numerous figures of men and women, and towards the left, above the head of some Bodhisatva or other great saint, is a sort of pyramid of circular segments, that may be intended for a mountain pinnacle, or flames, or something else.

X. Above the left door is a man asleep; and a female and another figure, both half nude talking together. Then to the left is another man lying on a couch, while a bald old man sits in front, and a female is directing the attention of the one to the other.

To the left of the door are bits of figures.

XI. Between the doors of the cells inside have been figures; and all along the upper parts of the walls a good deal of decorative painting in creepers (*vêli*) is still left on a green ground.

It would be well worth while if Mr. Griffiths could be spared with a few students for some months to preserve a pictorial record of these remains, before they are for ever lost.

APPENDIX A.

THE BAUDDHA MYTHOLOGY OF NEPAL.

Pandit Bhagvanlâl Indraji* has supplied the following information on the modern Buddhism and mythology of Nepal, which may be helpful in illustrating what we find in the caves of Western India. The illustrations accompanying it are fac-similes from a series he had prepared in Nepal.

In Nepal the Buddhist images are divided into two kinds:—The *bâhya*, and *abhyantara* or *guhya*—those which are exposed and those which are secreted, that is of the exoteric and esoteric schools or rather of those who have accepted the *dîkshâ* or initiation of S'âkya in its simplicity and of those who, originally gained over from Tantric forms of Hinduism, accepted what is called the *abhyantara* or *Mahâyâna dîkshâ* and whose images are accessible only to those of the sect. Those of the *S'âkya dîkshâ* generally accept the ceremonial and customs of the *Hinâyâna* school of Buddhists and after receiving the dîkshâ leave their families, 3, 12 or 30 days and live separately in a vihâra, abjure animal food, liquor, &c., and live in perfect continence, as bhikshus on the food given them in alms, and while they begging constantly ring a bell hung round their necks that they may not hear any worldly sound; meanwhile they read and study religion. At the end of this time, the neophyte usually goes to the priest saying 'the way of the S'âkya dîkshâ is very hard and the *Bhikshucharyâ* is not suited to him, and asks him to point out an easier way.' The priest accommodates him in this by recommending the *Mahâyâna dîkshâ* and to walk in the *kaula mârga* (or family life) which is the very opposite of the original teaching of Buddha, and violates every law of decency and morality. The mental repose, morality, temperance, inculcated in the Bauddha books are totally ignored or cast aside by this sect. The *Abhyantara* books, images, and customs are thus kept secret and are never spoken of to those of any other sect, while their temples are quite distinct.

The Bâhya or S'âkyamaṭa temples are called *bahâla* and *bahi*. *Bahâla* is a corruption of *vihâra*, and *bahi* means 'outside.' The original of this latter name being that the true Bhikshus of the S'âkyamaṭas finding the vihâras occupied by those who followed their *dîkshâ* only for a few days and spent their lives as followers of the *abhyantara dîkshâ*; they found themselves *outside* such monasteries and established others of their own to which they gave the name of *bahi*. Now, however, both *bahâla* and *bahi* are alike and both sects have assimilated to one other, the wives and children of the devotees living with them in the *bahâlas* and *bahis*; no such thing as continence is required, and a knowledge of the religion is almost unknown, though they call themselves *Bhikshus* they carry on all the usual trades. There is still a difference, however, between *bahâlas* and *bahis*, by which they may be distinguished: in the former the *Vajrachâryas* and *S'âkyabhikshus* reside, and in the latter *Bhikshus* and *Chailakas*.†

When the *Guhyas* have a separate temple of their own which, however, is seldom the case, it is called a *Guhyaprasâda*; in other cases they have a portion of the *vihâra* set apart often in an upper floor from which all others are excluded. The *bahâlas* and *bahis* have generally a ground plan similar to that of the Bauddha Cave vihâras, of about the 6th century, a court in front, and a shrine or temple at the back—of two or three storeys in height, the principal image being in it; and round the sides of the Court are smaller shrines of one or two storeys, in the lower storey of which are images; and the devotees live above. The principal image is usually Buddha, Avalôkitêśvara, or Dipankara. In the middle of the court is a *Chaitya*,—called *dharmadhâtu chaitya*, and images of Avalôkitês'vara, and other Bodhisatvas, Târâ and other *dêvîs*, Buddha, &c., both in the area and cells: *chaityas* and pillars for images are only in the area, as also the *dharma dhâtu Maṇḍala*.

---

* I should not omit to mention that, besides preparing fac-similes of the Ajantâ inscriptions for the preceding paper, the Pandit proved himself most useful in making out the details of the wall pictures, everyone of which he went over most carefully with me; and in writing out the notes, I usually left to him the order in which the different parts of each picture were to be noticed.

† The Bauddhas are all called *Bândas*, that is 'shaven,' of which there are four sects—*Vajracharyas, Sâkyabhikhus, Bhikshus*, and *Cha ilakas*.

The images are all *Bâhya* or *S'âkyamata*, and are such as are found in the later cave temples, *e.g.* Buddha, Avalôkitêśvara, Manjuśrî, Târâ, and other Bodhisatvas.

They are divided into three classes—

1. Buddha.
2. Bodhisatvas or Lôkêśvaras.
3. The S'aktîs and Dêvas.

The Nepalese believe that the world originates from Buddha. It is destroyed at the end of a long cycle, and what is left is Buddha as a germ, in which the wish arises to recreate the world, and this produces wind, and from the wind is produced water, and in it is a seven-fold *kamala* or lotos, and from this comes Adibuddha, the cause of all. (See fig 1.) From him arises the five Jnyânâtmaka Buddhas (or forms of the 'senses.')

1. Vairochana;
2. Akshobhya;
3. Ratnasambhava;
4. Amitâbha; and
5. Amoghasiddhi;

Which have five *śaktîs*,—1 Vajradhâtvîśvarî; 2 Lochanî; 3 Mâmakî; 4 Pândurâ; and 5 Târâ. These five produce five *Lôkêśvaras*—1 Samantabhadra; 2 Vajrapânî; 3 Ratnapânî; 4 Padmapânî; and 6 Visvapânî. Of these Padmapânî, by his power (*śâkti*) produced the Dêvas,—Indra, Brahmâ, and the other gods, and by these the world was made. S'âkyamuni and the other preceding Buddhas were *ansas*—a sort of *avatâras* of Âdibudha, and had appeared many times in the world before each attained to Buddhahood and then returned into Adibuddha, just as the cloud distils its water on the earth and after serving the ends of nature, again returns to clouds. All past Buddhas are thus called Tathâgata, as having so come (*âgatâ*), and so returned *yathâ âgatas tathâ gatah.* Bodhisatvas are those men who, not yet having attained to Buddhahood, are living so as to prepare for that. In Nepal, however, they are regarded as gods (*dêvas*), and, as possessed of supernatural powers, they are very numerous, and are called Lôkêśvaras:—among these Arya Avalôkitêśvara or Padmapânî Lôkêśvara is the chief.

The powers—*S'âkti*—of Buddha are personified as *dêvîs*, of which Târâ stands first. The Brahmanical gods Brahmâ, Indra, Vishnu, &c., are recognized as subsidiary to Buddha and the Bodhisatvas. To Gaṇêśa, Bhairava, Mahâkâla, Kubêra, &c., they pay reverence; but their images are never found in the Vihâras.

The Dêvas of the Guhyas are very numerous, among which Buddha, the Bodhisatvas, S'aktîs, &c., have a place, but under different forms (*rûpas*)—horrible and obscene, the Buddhas and Bodhisatvas being represented in the embraces of their respective S'aktîs as Vajrasatva (in fig. 31 and in fig. 32),—and in a variety of styles, each being recognized by the *chinha*. The S'aktîs are also represented naked and in obscene attitudes. Among their chief divinities are Vajradhara (fig. 24) and Akshobhya.

The figures, illustrative of this mythology on the accompanying plates, were selected from among many others in Nepalese books and Vihâras, and copied with care. The painters in Nepal, however, are not mythologists and only copy faithfully what they have before them, but have departed gradually so far from the originals, as in painting to represent their male divinities as females (*e. g.*, figs. 1, 3, 14, 15, 23, &c.); in the images of metal, &c., however, this mistake is not made.

The following are the divinities represented:—

FIG. 1.

Âdibuddha.

The first cause of the five Buddhas, on the lotos springing from the waters, with light emanating from his body and a *bhâmaṇḍala* or glory round his head.

FIG. 2.

Ratnatraya consisting of Buddha, Dharma, and Sangha.

'The three jewels' of religion,—that is Buddha, the Law, and the Assembly. These correspond respectively to Buddha, or the *Chaitya*, the Wheel, and the Lion, in the early caves. In Nepal the image of Buddha in this case is represented by that of Akshobhya whose *mudrâ* is the *bhûmisparśa* or that in which Buddha sat under the *Bodhi* tree.

1 ADIBUDDHA

2 RATNATRAYA
DHARMA BUDDHA SANGHA

3 DÎPANKARA TATHÂGATA

4 BUDDHA (VAJRÂSANA BHATTÂRKA)

Govt. Photozincographic Office, Poona 1879.

5 BUDDHA ŚĀKYAMUNI

6 VAIROCHANA BUDDHA

7 AKSHOBHYA BUDDHA

8 RATNASAMBHAVA BUDDHA

9 AMITÂBHA BUDDHA

10 AMOGHASIDDHI BUDDHA

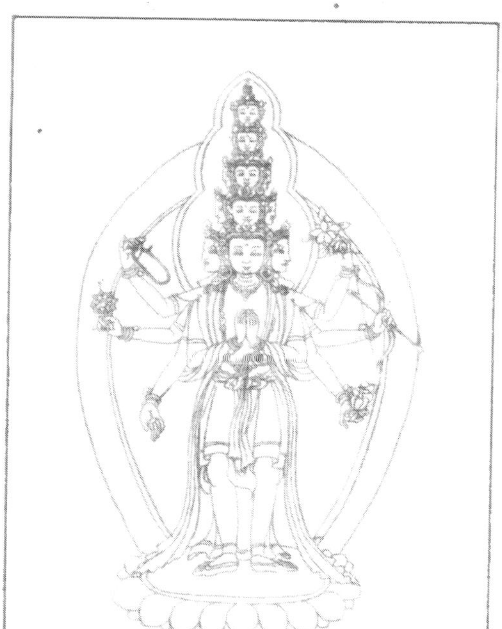

11 AVALOKITEŚVARA (SAHASRABÂHULOKESVARA)

12 LOCHINÎ ÂRYA AVALOKITEŚVARA TÂRÂ

13 PADMAPÂNI LOKEŚVARA

14 CHINTÂMANI LOKEŚVARA

15 SIMHANÂTHA LOKEŚVARA

16 AMOGHAPÂŚA LOKEŚVARA

Plate XXVI

17

18 MANJUŚRÎ

19

20

21

22

23 VAJRASATVA

24 VAJRADHARA

25 ARYA TÂRÂ

26 PRAJNÂPÂRAMITÂ

27 APARIMITÂ

28 VASUDHÂRÂ

Plate XXIX.

29 KUBÊRA

30 MAHÂKÂLA

31

32

37

38

CHAITYAS

39

40

For *Dharma* the image is called Prajnâpâramitâ from the name of a sacred book of which it may be regarded as the feminine personification, with four hands, the upper left holding a *kamala* on which lies the book; in the upper right a *mâlâ* or rosary, and the lower are in the *dharmachakra mudrâ*, or teaching attitude. *Sangha* is a male personification of the Assembly with four hands, in the upper left is a lotos and in the right a lotos, and with the other two he makes *namaskâra*.

FIG. 3.

Dipankara Tathagata.

The Nepalese place this Buddha in the fifty-second place among the fifty-five, they reckon back before Śâkya Muni, and the Sinhalese in the twenty-fourth. He is much worshipped. In Bhâtgâon, the greatest of the vihâras is dedicated to him, and contain a gigantic clay image of him. When the ceremonies of *Sanghabhojana* and *Yugâdidâna* are performed, a large metal image of Dîpankara is made for worship and is afterwards placed in the vihâra of the sect to which the celebrator belongs. Thus his images are multiplied. Two bhikshus are always represented beside him, holding a rod (or crozier), called *khikkharikâ*, in Nepal, two cubits in length, coloured red and yellow, with a circle at the top round a figure of Buddha or a *Chaitya*, and in the left hand a brass alms-bowl with a small mouth.

FIG. 4.

Buddha.

Vajrâsana Bhaṭṭârka the name of Buddha when he went to sit under the Bodhi tree, where his hands are represented in the *Bhûsparśa mudrâ*. On his right is Maitreya Bodhisatva, with an image of Buddha on his head, a *naga-champâ* flower in his left hand and a *châmara* in his right. On the other side is Lôkêśvara, Bodhisatva, a *kamala* flower in his left hand and a *châmara* in his right.

FIG. 5.

Buddha Śâkyamuni.

Buddha Śâkyamuni is the image of Gautama, an *avatâra* of the deity; his right hand held up in the *abhaya mudrâ*, with the left hand he holds up his robe.

FIGS. 6 to 10.

Panchajnânâtmaka Buddha.

These are believed to be forms of the five senses: feeling, smelling, &c. They are distinguished from each other by the peculiar manner of holding hands, which is called *mudrâs*. In all other respects their general attitude is the same. Sometimes the feet of their couches are figures of certain animals and birds peculiar to each of them, by which means they may also be distinguished from each other. Besides these, in painting, each has his own colour. The following is a table showing the above in detail:—

Names of Buddha.	*Mudra* or mode of holding the hands.	Animal or Birds on their couches.	Colour.
Vairochâna.	Dharmachakra (wheel of religion.)	Lion.	White.
Akshobhya.	Bhumisparśa (touching the floor).	Elephant.	Green.
Ratna Sambhava.	Vara (blessing).	Horse.	Yellow.
Amitâbha.	Dhyâna (mental contemplation).	Peacock.	Red.
Amoghasiddhi.	Abhaya (blessing of fearlessness.	Eagle.	Black.

The images of these five Buddhas are sometimes carried or painted in Vihâras, gateways of houses and such other places, in which case they are either figured in the above order or one at each corner and Vairochana in the centre. On chaityas they are also figured at the corners with the exception of that of Vairochana, which is then believed to be enshrined in the Chaitya.

Among Guhya or Abhyantara sects, the figures of these five Buddhas are very peculiar. In order to distinguish them, to each is allotted certain signs which are held by them in their hands. These signs are given below :—

Names of Signs.	Name of Buddhas.
Chakra (wheel).	Vairochana.
Vajru (Thunderbolt).	Aksobhya.
Ratna (Jewel).	Ratnasambhava.
Rakta Padma (Red lotus).	Amitâbha.
Viśva Vajra (Thunderbolt having four points on four end).	Amoghasiddhi.

FIG. 11.

Sahasra Bâhu Lôkêśvara.

This is also one of the several forms of Avalôkitêśvara. A beautiful metal idol of this Buddha is put up on the gateway of the temple called the Ârya Avalôkitêśara Vihâra, or commonly known by the people by the name of Machhendra Bahâla at Kâtmându. The difference between this figure and that is that besides eight hands shown in this, it has also several other hands represented around it.

FIG. 12.

Ârya Avalôkitêśvara.

This is known by people of other than the Bauddha religion as Machhendranâtha, the pupil or follower of Gorakshanâtha. The Bauddhas believe Gorakshanâtha to have been a disciple of Avalôkitêśvara. This figure has a lotos in his left hand and the right is held in the attitude of giving a blessing, sometimes it is also figured with the images of Lochanî and Târâ on either side, as shown in this instance. The worship of Avalôkitêśvara exists to a considerable extent in Nepal and fairs are held in his honour, when the car of this idol is dragged round the whole city with great eclât and honour. He has a large temple at Lâlitapaṭṭana also, where fairs are also held in its honour and a car is dragged round the town. After the car feast, the idol is removed to a large village called Bungamati, situate at a distance of 3½ miles towards the south of Lâlitapaṭṭana, where it is kept for six months, and then brought back to Lâlitapaṭṭana again. The idols of the vihâras of Kâtmându and Paṭṭan are made of clay and their feet of silver, and it is a general belief that they contain a pitcher of *amṛita* (nectar) in them. The idols are always properly covered with clothes and silver and gold ornaments.

Avalôkitêśvara is regarded as the chief among Bodhisatvas. They possess superhuman powers, are very kind and compassionate and save people from their sins, and by seeking refuge from them, people may be relieved from all miseries and pains.

FIG. 13.

Padmapânî Lôkêśvara.

Is also called Karunârṇava (ocean of mercy), and is one of the forms of Avalôkitêśvara. It is believed to be the form Avalôkitêśvara took at the time when he went to relieve sinners in the great hell. He holds a lotos in his hand, over which is put a vessel of *Amṛita* (nectar).

FIG. 14.

Chintâmani Lôkêśvara.

He is a Bodhisatva, believed to be the donor of everything desired by his worshippers, so every one desirous of any thing worships him. Figures of him are generally seen painted on the walls of the houses of Kâtmându, as well as in the side rooms of some of the Vihâras.

He is represented as standing under the tree *Kalpa Vriksa* and a worshipper stands before him, apparently in the attitude of begging, to whom he gives jewels, picking them from the tree.

FIG. 15.

Simhanâtha Lôkêśvara.

He is also a Bodhisatva, worshipped with a view to gaining success in wars; and for safety from the fears of foes. The mode in which he is sitting is called *Mahârâjalila.* He is represented as sitting on a lion in the above way. (The Nepalese always make poor figures of lions never having seen them ; it is so in this case also). He wears the skin of a deer on his left shoulder ; on his head, among his hair, are a moon and a skull. On his right is a trident with a serpent wound round it, and on his left is placed a sword on a lotos ; this sword is called *Chandrahâsa Khadaga.*

A life size figure of this kind is placed on a stone column 12 feet high in the yard of the Machhendra Vihâra at Kâtmându.

FIG. 16.

Amoghapâśa Lôkêśvara.

He is also a Bodhisatva, worshipped for release from prison and from great distress. He has eight hands, on the right side, the first, from below, is held in *Tarka Mudrâ* (mode of thinking), the second in mode of blessing, the third holds a snare, and the fourth a rosary (*mâlâ*). On the left side the first hand holds a vessel of nectar, the second a red lotos, the third a trident, and the fourth a book, called *Prajnapârâmitâ.*

FIG. 17.

Avalôkitêśvara.

This is one of his forms. His right hand is in the *mudrâ* of blessing, and with his left hand he holds a lotus, he is sitting under an Aśoka tree.

FIG. 18.

Manjuśrî.

This is a male figure ; he is also considered a Bodhisatva or Lôkêśvara. With his right hand he holds the Chandrahâsa Khadaga, with the left hand the book *Prajnâpâramita* placed on a lotus. He is worshipped by people desirous of acquiring *Vidya* or education. He is well known in Nepal, and figures of him are to be seen everywhere. The chief place of his worship is considered to be on a hill behind that on which is built the principal chaitya of Nepal, called Svayambhûnâtha. Of him it is related that formerly the valley of Nepal was filled with water which he cleared out and made it habitable for men.

FIG. 19.

Jânguli Târâ.

This is a female figure and is seated on a corpse. She has four hands. The upper right hand holds a white serpent ; by the left she gives a blessing ; and the other two hands are engaged in playing on a *Vinâ* or Bin. In painting she is always represented of a white colour.

FIG. 20.

Hâlâhala Lôkêśvara.

This is an idol of the Guhya sect. It has three heads, covered with a crown, which carries a figure of Amitâbha and the moon. It has eight hands. On the right side the first from above, holds a circle, the second a bow, the third a trident, on which is wound a serpent, and the fourth is in the *mudrâ* of blessing. On the left side the first holds a flower, the second draws the bow held in the other hand, the third a skull filled with flowers, and the fourth an *ankuśa* or elephant-goad. He wears the skin of a lion, and in his lap is seated his Śakti (wife).

FIG. 21.

Hâlâhala Lôkêśvara.

This is another form of the same Lôkêśvara, the difference simply being in his having six-hands in this, instead of sight, as on No. 20; owing to shortness of two hands, the lotus and the trident are placed by his side. In place of the skull filled with flowers, here is simply a flower. This idol is sometimes seen among the Bâhya sect.

FIG. 22.

Kâranḍa Vyûha Lôkêśvara.

He is worshipped as a Bodhisatva among the Guhya sect.

FIG. 23.

Vajrasatva.

He is considered a portion of Adi-Buddha, and is believed to be the teacher of all; he is seated in the mode called the *Padmâsana mudrâ*; he balances a thunderbolt on the tip of the third finger of his right hand, and with his left hand he holds a bell.

FIG. 24.

Vajradhârâ.

Vajradhara is a chief teacher of the Abhyantara sect, and is believed to be a fragment of Adi-Buddha and originator of *Mahayâna* or *Kaula* branch of the religion. He holds a thunderbolt in his right hand and a bell in his left.

FIG. 25.

Arya Tárá.

Among the female deities, this idol has the most renown in Nepal. She has her images of different forms, both among the Guhya and Bâhya sects. This figure belongs to the Bâhyas. Her left hand holds a lotus and the right is in the attitude of blessing.

FIG. 26.

Prajnâpâramitâ.

This is a female figure: men desirous of knowing the true religion, worship her.

FIG. 27.

Aparimitâ.

This is also a female figure. By the mistake of the painter it is represented as a male. She has a vessel of nectar in her lap. People desirous of long life, worship her.

FIG. 28.

Vasudhârâ.

Vasudhârâ is the Lakshmî of the Bauddhas and is worshipped for acquiring money. She is figured in various forms; sometimes she is represented with three faces and driving a car drawn by seven boars. This idol is worshipped by the Jainas in these later times. The Jainas have a verse composed in her praise which they repeat on every Divâli day. The verse is called *Vasudhârâ*. The Jainas themselves admit that this belonged to the Bauddhas.

Her figure has six hands. On the right side, the first from above, holds a circle, the second a lute, and the third is in the *mudrâ* of bestowing a blessing. On the left side, the first holds a book, the second a bunch of grain, and a vessel of nectar is placed in her lap.

FIG. 29.

Kubêra.

The Nepalese call him by the name of Jambala. He is represented as a fat, big-bellied, grave-faced figure, and is believed to be the master of wealth. He has a mungoose in his left hand and a citron in his right. He is worshipped for the protection of wealth.

FIG. 30.

Mahâkâla.

This is a dreadful, awe-inspiring, naked male figure. The hair on the head is curly and stands upright. His mouth is wide open with the teeth visible. He is represented as dancing on a corpse with a serpent wound round his neck. With his right hand he holds a cup, made of a human skull and filled with blood, he holds a mangoose with his left hand, and around him are flames of fire.

He is worshipped with the desire to be saved from the fear of death and disease. In the eastern part of Kâtmându there is a temple of Mahâkâla where there is a figure of him 12 feet high in this form. The floor and walls of his temple are always dyed with the blood of goats, fowls, &c., killed for him on the spot.

FIG. 31.

This a combined figure of S'akti and Vajradhârâ of Fig. 24. He is represented in union with his *S'akti*, and holds a thunderbolt in his right hand and a bell in his left.

FIG. 32.

Vairochana.

This is a figure of Vairochana as worshipped by the Abhyantara sect. He has a wheel in his hand, by which he is known. There are similar figures of the other four Buddhas, the difference being only in the objects they hold in their hands.

The Yoginîs.

The Yoginîs are believed to be six in number. Their names are—1 Vajrayoginî, 2 Maniyoginî, 3 Dhvajayoginî, 4 Âdarśayoginî, 5 Pichchayoginî, and 6 Pushpayoginî. These names are given to them from the names of the different objects they hold in their right hands; such as the *vajra*, or thunderbolt, *maṇi* or jewel, *âdarśa* or a looking glass, *pichcha* or feather, and *pushpa* or flower. In all other respects they are similar. All of them, in their left hands, hold a skull filled with blood, bowels, &c. They wear strings of human heads around their necks, one foot is raised apparently in the act of dancing; they hold a staff in one of their hands and on the top of the staff is a vessel, over which are three human heads, one above the other, surmounted by a trident. The figures are encircled by flames.

These Yoginîs are worshipped by people of the Brahmanical religion, also in Nepal. A temple of Vajrayoginî is situated on a hill six miles to the east of Kâtmându. The idol in this temple, however, is not naked, but is covered with clothes and ornaments.

FIGS. 37 TO 40.

Chaityas.

There are very many Chaityas in Nepal. These are of all sizes, and are seen in streets and all places. They may he divided into three classes—one class being the ancient, a second those of an earlier date than 300 years ago, and the third of modern times. The ancient ones are similar to those of Sânchi and surrounding places, built in the times of Aśoka, the difference simply being that in these *Chaityas* the capitals are tall, which is not the case among the latter. The Svayambhunâtha Khâsâ-chaitya, Kâthesambhu, and the four great chaityas surrounding Lalitapaṭṭana, may be placed in this class.

The second class of Chaityas are built of brick, and resembles somewhat those in the Caves of about the sixth century. There are very few in Nepal; one is situate on the bank of the Vishṇumâtî, and another at a little distance from a *praṇalî* or water spring of king Anśuvarmâ.

Those of the third class are made of stone and are of modern construction. They are of various styled, four of which are given in the plate as samples.

APPENDIX B.

Sanscrit Inscription from Cintra.

The accompanying plate is a slightly reduced photo-lithograph from one in Murphy's *Travels in Portugal* (1795), where it is said to be one of two—carried by Don John de Castro from India,—to be seen in his garden at Cintra (see pp. 274, 279). It might be expected that one of these inscriptions would be that carried off from Elephanta: but it is not this one, which Bhgavanlâl Indraji believes rather to have been taken from Somanâtha Paṭṭan. The rough translation given by Sir Charles Wilkins in Murphy's work is of no value, and the transcript on the plate, having been made by a person quite ignorant of Sanscrit, contains many errors. Some of these the Pandit has been able to correct in the following transcript with considerable confidence, but there are others regarding which he is in doubt as to the correct reading.

It is dated in the Vikrama Samvat era 1343, 5th Mâgha Śuda, on which day Gaṇḍa Tripurântaka, a Pâśupata, dedicated a temple to Tripurântakeśvara. Besides this he had built other temples at Somanâtha Pâṭṭan. It is interesting as making mention of Gaṇḍa Bhâva Bṛihaspati (who lived in the time of Kumârapâla) having established an image of a Nakulîśpâśapata Achârya there; and thus takes occasion to give the genealogy of the heads of the Nakulîśapâśupata sect. In the preface it gives the genealogy of Sâranga Deva of Gujarât, in whose reign the temple was built. And in the latter part are some curious details relating to the worship and management of the temples of that age. The Pandit intends to translate it in full for publication in the *Indian Antiquary*.

The Inscription is produced here to direct attention to it, and if possible to lead to the securing of a good rubbing, impression, or photograph of the original.

Transcript by Bhagvanlâl Indraji Pandit.

॥ ॐनमः शिवाय ॥

ऋदिस्थितं चिन्मयमात्मवेदिनः
समाधिमास्थाय विलोकयंति यं
स त्रैविधं तापमपाकरोतु वः
स्तनंध्ययः श्वेतमयूखभूषणः ॥ १ ॥
शैलात्मजोरसिजशृंगकुरंगनाभि-
पत्रावलीतलिनतल्पशयालुपाणिः
पीयूषभानुकलिकाकलितावतंसो
देवः शिवानि वितनोतु दिवानिशं वः ॥ २ ॥
त्रैलोक्यमंगलमनंगरिपोरपत्य-
मंकूरितैकदशनो लसदानश्रीः
देवः प्रपन्नहृदयैकपदीं कपर्दी
भूयादनेकपमुखः सुखसंपदे नः ॥ ३ ॥

Sanskrit Inscription in the garden of Don John de Castro at Cintra in Portugal.

Govt. Photozincographic Office, Poona, 1879.

श्रीविश्वमल्ल इति भूपतिमौलिरत्नं
चौलुक्यवंशमवतंसयति स्म जिष्णुः
यस्य त्रिधामपि संयति मण्डलाग्र-
मारादमंस्त शतधारमरातिवर्गः ॥ ४ ॥
आबद्धमूलमभितः क्षितिपाद्रिजात-
मुन्मूलयन्कुलिशवंशभुवा भुजेन
सत्वस्य यः किमपि धाम जनेन राज
नारायणेति जगदे जगदेकनाथः ॥ ५ ॥
यस्मिन्नायकतां व्यधत्त सकले क्षत्रावतंसे जग-
त्तापव्यापदपाकरिष्णुमहिमा श्रीवैद्यनाथःप्रभुः ।
शश्वत्तेन चिकित्सिता स्तदुचितं विश्वोपकार व्रत-
स्नातेन प्रतिभूभुजामपि इदः प्रौढामदग्रन्थयः ॥ ६ ॥
नागल्लदेवीति बभूव यस्य
जाया जयश्रीरिव देहबद्धा
तया स राजा सुतरां बभासे
भासेव देवो हरिणांकमूर्त्तिः ॥ ७ ॥
आशान्तविख्यातभुजप्रतापः
प्रतापमल्लावरजः स राजा
स्वपौरुषोत्कर्षरसातिरेका-
देकातपत्रां बुभुजे धरित्रीम् ॥ ८ ॥
श्रीविश्वमल्लः स्वपदे भिषिच्य
प्रतापमल्लात्मजमर्जुनं सः
साकं सुधापाकमभुंक्त (नाक)
नितम्बिनीनामधरामृतेन ॥ ९ ॥
राकानिशाकरसनाभिगुणाभिरामो
दामोदरांशइवविक्रममांसलश्रीः
भूपालमौलिमणिरर्जुनदेवनामा
कामार्जुनीमिव धनानि धरामदुग्ध ॥ १० ॥
हस्ते विधाय कदनाय दुराशयानां
दानावधूतसुरशाखिनि भूमिचक्रं
यः स्वैरुदारचरितैरनघः प्रजानां
रक्षां चकार किल चक्रधरावतारः ॥११॥
तस्यांगभूर्ज्जयति गुर्ज्जरराजलक्ष्मी-
संभोगकन्दालितमौग्ध्यविमग्नचेताः
क्षोणीसमुद्धरणकेलिरसोत्तरंगः

सारंगदेव इति शार्ङ्गधरानुभावः ॥१२॥
युधियादवमालवेश्वराबकृतक्षीणवलीबलेनयः
पृथुविग्रहधारिणौ पुरा
पतगेन्द्रोगजकच्छपाविव ॥१३॥
॥ इतश्च ॥
भट्टारकश्रीलकुलीशमूर्त्या
तपःक्रियाकाण्डफलप्रदाता ॥
अवातरद्विश्वमनुग्रहीतुं
देवः स्वयं बालमृगांकमौलिः ॥ १४ ॥
अनुग्रहीतुं च चिरांविपुत्रका
नुलूकभूतानभिशापतः पितुः ॥
ललाटमुर्ध्या इव लाटभूषणं
समेत्यकराजणमध्युवासतः १५ ॥
आवर्तेरुश्चत्वारः पाशुपतव्रतविशेषवृद्ध्यर्थं
इह कुशिकगार्ग्यकारुषमैत्रेया इति तदंतसदः ॥ १६ ॥
ततस्तपस्विनामेषा चतुर्द्धा जातिरुद्गता ॥
भुवं विभूषयामास चतुर्णवमुद्रिताम् ॥ १७ ॥
एतै रनुगृहीतानामन्वयानां महात्मनां ।
निः सीमवैभवं श्री — — कामित्यभूत् ॥ १८ ॥
गार्ग्येयगोत्राभरणं बभूव
स्थानाधिपः कार्तिकराशिनामा ॥
मूर्तस्तपोराशिरिवाश्रितानां–
मालोकमात्रेण हरन्नघौघान् ॥ १९ ॥
तेन स्व हस्तकमलानुगृहीतजन्मा
वाल्मीकिराशिरुदियाय दयालुचेताः ॥
वाणीवर्तार्थपदवी — — पद्मानां
न्यासैः स्वबित्तावि म — — नः पुनातः ॥ २० ॥
तेनानुगृह्य समकोति सतां प्रबोध
कारी तपोधनयुवा त्रिपुरान्तकोति
साक्षाद्भवान्ति विबुधाः किलतद्विधानां
हस्तांबुजेन दृषदोऽपि कृतप्रतिष्ठाः ॥ २१ ॥
वाल्मीकिराशेः सुगृहीतनाम्न-
स्तस्यैवाशिष्यस्त्रिपुरान्तकेति
तीर्थान्तरालोकनकौतुकेन
पवित्रयामासदिशश्चतस्रः ॥ २२ ॥
पूर्वंतपस्विगृहिणीस्पृहणीयमूर्ति–

योदेवदारुविपिनेविजहारदेवः
आशावधूक्वणिमानमनुगृहीतुं
तीर्थावगाहनमिषेण चचारसोयं ॥ २३ ॥
समाधिपूतेन हृदांबुजेन
यः — — — — — —
ततः शुचिवल्लसरः सरोजै
रानर्च केदारपदारविन्दे ॥ २४ ॥
जगद्गुरुं चेतसि यः प्रपद्य
योगेश्वरं मूर्त्तमि — — — —
— — — — — — प्रसाद
संपत्तिलभ्यानि तपः फलानि ॥ २५ ॥
मिथोमिलज्जन्हुकलिन्दकन्या.
तरंगहस्तोपहृतैः पयोभिः
ममज्जयचा — — — — — —
– – – –·– षः पादामिवप्रयागः ॥२६॥
प्रदक्षणीकृत्य सतां प्रदीपः
श्रीपर्वते यः किल सर्वतोपि
श्रीमल्लिनाथस्य विलोकनेन
कृतार्थ – – – – – – त्ते ॥२७॥
प्रेंखोल्लितानि कलशोद्भवपादमुद्रा–
निः कल्मषाकृतिषु विन्ध्यगिरेः शिलासु
रेवाजलानि गजराजविगाहलीलां
– – – – – – पाण्यपियः सिषेवे ॥२८॥
गोदावरीतीरवि(हा)रिणीभि-
र्वनस्थलीनामधिदेवताभिः
कृतार्थयन्नद्यसदृक्प्रयोजं
यो जंगमस्येव – – – – – – ॥२९॥
ततः शमाद्वैतरसाभिरामे।
रामेश्वरं चेतसि चिन्तयन् यः
ददर्श लंकाधिपकालरात्रेः
प्रस्थानवीथीमिव सेतुलेखाम् ॥३०॥
श्रीदेवपत्तनसमस्तघनस्तनीनां
नेत्रारविन्दसुकृतैरिव सानुबंधैः
तीर्थावगाहनधिया दिशिपश्चिमाया-
मायातवानुपशमायतनं कृती वः ॥३१॥
सरस्वतीसागरसंप्रयोग
विभूषिताभोगमथागमद्यः

सोमेशचूडाचलमानबाल-
चंद्रप्रभासंवलितं प्रभासं ॥३२॥
इह महीतलतीर्थविगाहना
दखिलतीर्थमयीं दधदाकार्तिं ॥
भुवनभूषणभूतमभूषय–
न्नगरमिन्दुकलाभरणस्ययः ॥ ३३ ॥
इहसाक्षादुमाकान्तः श्रीमान्गंडवृहस्पातिः ।
आर्यमेनं विनिर्म्माय प(दं)चक्रेमहत्तरं ॥३४॥
स्थानकं निजविशुद्धचरित्रै-
रुद्धरिष्यति महत्तर एषः
इत्यवेत्य मुमुदे हृदि –
– – – – प्रणजातरसेन ॥३५॥
आस्ति श्रीत्रिपुरान्तकोपि विवुधश्रेणीकिरीटोपल
च्छायापल्लवलालितांघ्रिकमलः कामाभिरामध्वनिः
यस्योद्दामचरित्रवैभवनिधेरेषा कियंतंगुण
ग्रामं धारयितुं स्वकुक्षिकुहरकोडे वराकी श्रुतिः ॥३६॥
धनानि कामाधिकवामलोचना-
विलोचनप्रांचलचंचलानि यः
ददौमहादौस्थ्यानिपीडितात्मने
सतां प्रपन्नार्त्तिहरा हि सम्पदः ॥३७॥
आस्थितस्य पुरुषोत्तमान्वये
कामजन्मनि समाहितबुद्धेः
यस्यपुण्यघटितस्य रमेति
प्रेयसी भुवनभूषणमास्ते ॥३८॥
सरस्वतीमौलिशयालुकेतकी-
पलाशलक्ष्मीसहपांशुकेलयः ॥
महात्मनो यस्य महोज्वला गुणाः ।
दिगंगनानामवतंसतां ययुः ॥३९॥
सोमेश्वरायतनमण्डपमुत्तरेण ।
श्रीभाजिजीर्णघटिकालयसन्निधाने
श्रीकंठपंचमुखवासमाधिश्रितानि ॥
येनाक्रियन्त कृतिना यतनानि पंच ॥४०॥
मातुर्म्माल्हणदेव्या यः श्रेयसे माल्हणेश्वरं
सतामध्येयमहिमा तन्मध्ये निरमापयत् ॥४१॥
उमापतेरायतनं नाम्ना गण्डबृहस्पतेः ।
कृती कृतयुगाचारः कारयामास तत्र यः ॥ ४२ ॥
श्री वृहस्पतिभार्यीया उमायाः श्लाघ्यजन्मनः ।

श्रेयसे यः सतांसीमा निरमासीदुमेश्वरं ॥४३॥
इहस्वनाम्ना त्रिपुरान्तकेश्वरं
महत्तरश्री त्रिपुरान्तको व्यधात् ।
प्रियाभिधानेन मनोरमश्रिया
रमापतिः संविदधे रमेश्वम् ॥४४॥
गोरक्षकं भैरवमांजनेयं
सरस्वतीं सिद्धिविनायकं च
चकार पंचायतनान्तराले
बालेन्दुमौलिस्थितमानसो यः ॥४५॥
आत्मबाहुयुगसौहृदान्वित-
स्तंभगौरवयुतं सुतोरणं
दूरमस्तदुरितस्तदुत्तर
द्वारभूपरिसरे चकार यः ॥४६॥
सम्पाउर्ज्जनाय देवानां कावडिद्वयमंभसः
सम्मार्जनी जगत्याश्च कोलिनी प्रतिवासरं ॥४७॥
कर्त्तव्यमेतदुभयं बटुकेन पटीयसा ॥
स्वमासपाटकद्रव्यनैवेद्याम्भोपयोगतः ॥४८॥ युग्मं ॥
श्रीखंडहेतोः शशिखंडमौलि
— — — — — — — पारकेयः
द्रम्मांश्चकार प्रतिमासमष्टा
वष्टापदोत्सर्गनिसर्गपूतः॥४९॥
दातव्यंमालिकश्रेण्या शतपत्रशतद्वयं ।
नवीनकणवीराणां द्वेसहस्रे च नित्यशः ॥५०॥
घटीवाहाय घाटिभ्यो गहीतुं शुचि — — कं
चक्रेपरीक्षिपट्टे यः षट्द्रम्मान्मासपाटके ॥५१॥
माणकद्वितयं चोषा मुद्रानामेकमाणकं
घृतं कर्षाश्च चत्वारस्तैलं दीपाय तादृशम् ॥५२॥
जात्यानि पंचपूगानि स्थितके स्थितिशालिना
कोष्टागारेषु (गण्डेन) प्रत्यहं येनचक्रिरे ॥ ५३ ॥ युग्मं ॥
इहैव धूपवेलार्थं गुग्गुलस्य मणद्वयं
यः पुण्येषु समासक्तः प्रातिमासमकारयत् ॥ ५४ ॥
(ततः सन) वपंचाशत्पत्राणि फणिवल्लिधाम् ।
मेहरेण प्रदेयानि नित्यं बीटकहेतवे ॥ ५५ ॥
पशुपालेन तदेवं धर्मस्थानोपहारसंबद्धं
श्री (सोमेश्वर) कोष्टागारादानीयदातव्यं ॥ ५६ ॥
चोषामाणकमेकं निर्व्वापे पवित्रकाद्वयं मुद्राः
नित्यं घृतकर्षौद्वाविति पशुपालाय दातव्यं ॥ ५७ ॥

...............दातव्यं नित्यनैवेद्यहेतवे ।
ततस्तदन्नं बटुना पचनीयं प्रयत्नतः ॥ ५८ ॥
पशुपालेन संकल्प्य तन्नैवेद्यं सबाटिकं ।
बटुकाय प्रदा(तव्यं पूजाक)र्मविधायिने ॥ ५९ ॥
मंडपिकायां स्थितके चातुर्जातकशासनात् ।
प्रत्यहं यः सतां सीमा द्रम्ममेकमकारयत् ॥ ६० ॥
अत्रैव कारयामास ....न्नुदारधीः॥
स्थितके योनवद्रम्मान् बटुकग्रासहेतवे ॥ ६१ ॥
पूजामप्रतिमां कर्तुं प्रतिमासमुपेयुषः
देयाः परेदशद्रमाः पशुपालस्य.......तः ॥ ६२ ॥
चातुर्जातकपाटानां यःसंमिलितपौत्तके
ततः पंचदशद्रम्मान् प्रतिमासं न्यधत्त यः ६३ ॥
हट्टानि योविशिष्टानि त्रोणि प्रीणितमानसः
चातुर्जातकपाटेभ्यो वित्तेनादाय दत्तवान् ॥ ६४ ॥
तेषां मध्यादुत्तमं हट्टमेकं.
देवश्रद्धाशालिना मालिकेभ्यः
नित्यं पूजापुष्पजातोपहारे
श्रीमच्चातुर्ज्जातकेन प्रदत्तं ॥ ६५ ॥
चैत्रीमहे भाद्रपदीमहे च
पावित्रकं विस्तरणं च कर्तुं
महाजनोपि प्रतिहट्टमेकं
द्रम्मं विशेषस्थितिके चकार ॥ ६६॥
कोष्ठागारेण पूगानि मेहरेण दलानिच
शिवरात्रौ प्रदेयानि चातुर्जातकबीटके ॥६७ ॥
श्री सोमनाथप्रभुराजपादिका—
त्रये त्रिभिर्हट्टवाणि ग्मिरात्मनां
स्नमालिकेराणि पुगांश्च कोमला
सदाविधेयानि विशुद्धबुद्धिभिः ॥ ६८ ॥
अमूनि सोमेश्वरदेवरीत्या
संपूज्य पंचायतनानि पूर्व्वं
अनेन पश्चात्पशुपालकेन
श्रीदेवपाद्यामधिरोहणीयं ॥ ६९ ॥
चैत्री भाद्रपदी भग्नपतितोद्धारहेतवे ।
चातुर्जातकपादेभ्यो धर्म्मस्थानमदत्तयः ॥ ७० ॥
स्वोपार्जितेन शुचिना विभवेन धर्म्म—
स्थानं चशासनमिदं च विनिर्म्ममेयः
तेनास्य कीर्तन निबद्धयशः पताका-

कारा मृगांकधवलाकृतिरुल्ललास ॥

श्रीगण्डराणकबृहस्पतिकीर्तनस्य
सारंगभूपतिसरस्तटभूषणास्य
यः श्रीविलासगृहमायतनस्य मध्ये
प्यात्मीयदेवकुलिकां रचयांचकार ॥ ७२ ॥

तादृग्विशेषशुचिताऽधिगमाय संतः
श्चित्तेषु बिभ्रतियदीयगुणाननस्रं ॥
पुष्णंति सिन्धुतनयाहृदयाधिनाथ
नाभीसरोरुहमृणालसनाभितंये ॥ ७३ ॥

निर्व्याजभक्तिरसवासितविश्वनाथ
माविभ्रतः सरिदभीकगनिरमंतः
एतस्य शारदतुषारमयूखलेखा
निःकल्मषाणि चरितानि जगत्पुनंति ॥ ७४ ॥

सोमार्कवत्कशशिमंडलतोनिपीय ।
पीयूषबद्धसखितानि तु भाषितानि ।
एषाप्रशस्ति रनवद्यपदार्थबन्धा
धंधात्मजेन विदधे धरणीधरेण ॥ ७५ ॥

एनां लिलेख मंत्री बिक्रमइति पूर्णसिंहभडजन्मा
उट्टंकयदथाशिल्पी नाहाडतनयश्चपूनसीह इति ॥
श्रीनृपविक्रमसं॰ १३४३ ॥ वर्षे माघशुदि ५ सोमेलिंग
प्रातिष्ठामहोत्सवः समजनि ॥